LOVE IN THE ECONOMY

Christopher McOustra

LOVE
IN THE ECONOMY

Catholic Social Doctrine
for the Individual

 St Paul Publications

St Paul Publications
Middlegreen, Slough SL3 6BT, England

Copyright © St Paul Publications 1990

ISBN 085439 324 2

Printed by The Guernsey Press Co., Guernsey C.I.

St Paul Publications is an activity of the priests and brothers
of the Society of St Paul who proclaim the Gospel through the media of
social communication.

Contents

Veni Sancte Spiritus
Et emitte caelitus
Lucis tuae radium

Veni Pater pauperum
Veni Dator munerum
Veni Lumen cordium

Come Holy Spirit
Send from heaven
A flash of your daylight

Come Father of the poor
Come Giver of gifts
Come Light of our hearts

Preface

In the summaries and extracts which follow Preface and Introduction, the reader will find teaching of the Catholic Church pertinent to the role of the individual in a modern economy. Teaching of the Catholic Church, may the reader please note: not pronouncements by this author. Author's comment is confined to the Introduction which follows this Preface and to the lesser introductions and notes to the Church documents treated.

Three key words in these documents are "responsibility", "justice", and "love". The third may be less often thought of than the first two, in the economy. The Introduction examines the character of this love, finds it clear-headed as well as compassionate, and suggests that it can and does both energize and humanize economic activity, for our own benefit, and for those in need.

The Church stresses the responsibilities of Catholics in particular, in the economy no less than in other departments of life. Accordingly this book has special point for Catholics: for laymen and women seeking to learn and live this Social Doctrine, as it is called; for workers in parish and diocese; for priests and teachers.

It may have interest for others too, whether Catholics or not: for students and teachers in secondary, tertiary and adult education; for men and women in business and at business schools; for trade unionists, and perhaps for economists, sociologists and politicians.

The writer seeks to focus on teaching relevant to Britain — his country, our country. This may prove helpful in other places also, to readers interested in ethics in a developed economy. And every human being, everywhere, participates in at least one aspect of economic life if in no other — the important aspect of consumption. So in a way, this book is for everyone.

In presenting only Catholic doctrine, no disrespect is intended to social teaching from Anglican and other Christian sources, nor to the work of economists, business people, trade unionists and others, within the Christian communion and outside it. Catholics acknowledge with gratitude a debt to all men and women of goodwill who advance our understanding. The volume and richness of Catholic social doctrine alone is however such as fully to employ this writer's capacities.

Laymen, laywomen, priests and religious have helped me in the work for this book. May I express my thanks to them all, especially to a hospitable and dear god-daughter, to the Catholic Truth Society for making the Vatican documents available in English, and to St Paul Publications.

Christopher McOustra

London
10 February 1990
Memoria of St Scholastica

Introduction

Catholic social doctrine

The best way to give an idea of Catholic social doctrine in the economic field may be to mention some of the matters the doctrine deals with. It deals with the right to private ownership, for example: ownership of home, possessions, investments, and businesses. It considers the responsibilities of ownership – the social mortgage.

The social doctrine considers the right to belong to a trade union, and responsibilities in the unions. It examines the rights and duties of employee and employer; pay and profit; profit-sharing, partnership, and share ownership; individual initiative, private enterprise, and competition. It reflects upon the primacy of human work, whether intellectual or manual, whether done in the family or outside; the subservient role of capital; poverty; economic imbalance; freedom and conscience; the need for moral and personal development in economic life, as well as technical advance; moral underdevelopment; the partnership with God and the fulfilment offered by the Holy Spirit through the work of Jesus Christ to every human being of goodwill, believer and unbeliever, in the economic aspects of life no less than in other aspects. It remembers the strengths offered in the Mass.

Through the Church's treatment of matters such as those instanced run certain key principles. One of these will be examined in a later section of this Introduction.

The material summarized or quoted, after the Introduction, is taken from the chief chapters of what the Catholic Church calls its modern social doctrine or teaching: from encyclicals and similar communications of popes from 1891 to date, and from work of the Second Vatican Council in the years 1962 to 1965. Material is also presented from statements by bishops in Rome and in Britain, from Church law, and from the final address given by Pope John Paul II when he visited Britain in 1982.

"Encyclical" is used in the Catholic Church to mean a letter from the Pope to his bishops throughout the world, or to the bishops and others. Like most papal documents, encyclicals are usually named and known by the first words of their official Latin text. The present work tries not to use unfamiliar Church words. It cannot avoid encyclical, however; and it retains the Latin titles.

Popes, Council and bishops have emphasized the importance of the social doctrine. "We must reaffirm most strongly that this Catholic social doctrine is an integral part of the Christian conception of life. It is our urgent desire that this doctrine be studied more and more..." (Pope John XXIII, 1961)[1] "Lay Christians... should acquire knowledge of social teaching especially..." (Second Vatican Council, 1965).[2] "As bishops, we should take urgent steps to encourage the study and development of the Church's social teaching, and to ensure that such teaching is treated as a priority in all programmes of adult education and formation. The social teachings of the Church must be recognized as an essential part of its doctrine and be presented in the upper forms of our secondary schools in a way which will instruct and inspire young people to assume their responsibilities in the community..." (bishops' Conference of England and Wales, 1980).[3]

The nature of the social doctrine is explained in several passages. The doctrine is not a "third way" between liberal capitalism and marxist collectivism, nor is it an ideology.[4] It has grown into a substantial volume of teaching, through the thick of developments such as the first industrial revolution and the inter-wars depression; through all the achievements and wretchednesses of the twentieth century. It examines principles for human situations that are sometimes profoundly difficult.

It would be surprising if such doctrine were blessed with total freedom from controversy. Theologians and others have debated – for example – the authority of teachings considered to be drawn from natural law, and on the other hand teachings drawn from understandings specifically Christian. They have debated the name: Is it really Doctrine, or just teaching?

The author does not dismiss such questions. His prime concern, however, within the special scope of the present work, is simply to put into their context the Church documents he treats, and objectively to summarize them. As to name, he notes the advice of the Vatican's Congregation for Catholic Education that "both stand for the same reality".[5] He uses "doctrine" here, "teaching" there, for change of sound.

Numbers preceded by § or §§ indicate the main paragraphs of the full texts, from which the shorter paragraphs or sections of the present work are composed. Numbers in brackets indicate secondary source-paragraphs.

There is a fair measure of repetition. Some of the problems and opportunities considered in 1891 are still with us. A writer can cut the repetition down, or can cut it out altogether, giving for each topic his own synthesis of the century's teaching. The present author has not done this: he offers the Church's doctrine as and when given.

The fact that a teaching is repeated across the years can be significant. The context, terms and tone of the repetition can be significant too: whether for example the teaching is repeated in the same or in different terms; and whether it is not so much repeated as developed.

Nor is the reader compelled to read the book from beginning to end. The teaching of the Second Vatican Council alone, or of a particular document, period or pope may satisfy. The reader may want to follow only one topic, pausing when signalled by a subheading – *Property* for example, or *Trade Unions* – or may want to use the index, where page-references to teachings and topics will be found.

May the facilities offered justify the pruning. As printed in the editions available in Britain, without preface, introductions or commentary, the twenty documents brought within the covers of the present work run to some 1,500 pages.

Selecting and summarizing – for which the author alone is responsible – cannot rival the authority of the full texts. Publishers and distributors of the full texts will be found in Annex 2, together with particulars of bookshops and libraries.

All teaching presented here is addressed by the Church with especial force to her own members. It has to be, for to the shame of those of us who are Catholics, some of us fail to live and work in accord with Christ's example as good as the accord many non-Catholics achieve.

The first document is Pope Leo XIII's encyclical *Rerum Novarum* of 1891, sometimes called The Workers' Charter. In splendid style Pope Leo addressed this "To His Venerable Brethren, all Patriarchs, Primates, Archbishops and Bishops of the Catholic World, in grace and communion with the Apostolic See". In his encyclical of 1931, Pius XI added "and to all the Faithful".

Always with respectfulness, the Church addresses much of her more recent teaching to non-Catholics as well as Catholics. In the text of *Mater et Magistra* in 1961 Pope John XXIII addressed "not only Our own sons and brothers, but also all men of goodwill".[6] From 1963 on, in text and on title page, the popes address most of their economic and social encyclicals to everyone of goodwill, as well as to Catholics. From 1979 they replace "all men of goodwill" by "all men and women of goodwill" or "all people".

The Second Vatican Council of 1962–65 likewise has words for everyone: "The Council addresses not only the sons of the Church and all who call upon the name of Christ, but the whole of humanity... The Council can find no more eloquent expression of its solidarity and respectful affection for the whole human family, to which it belongs, than to enter into dialogue with it..."[7]

People are surprised to learn that the Church concerns herself with the economy. The Church indeed disclaims authority to teach in technical matters outside her competence. She emphasizes the responsibility of the individuals and organizations involved.

The Catholic Church does however concern herself with Christian principle and practice in every department of life, including the economic. She also concerns herself with the nature of human beings, with our fulfilment, and with human society. In these studies she seeks to learn first and foremost from Jesus Christ. She also seeks to learn from human experience and science: from anthropology, history, philosophy, psychology, sociology, ethics, and economics; from the lives and work of men and women of all faiths and of none, through the centuries. The Church's teaching is thus a feast of foods many of which we ourselves have shared in providing, whether or not we acknowledge Christ, the guidance of the Holy Spirit, and the Church's place at the table; whether we are Catholics, or of some other faith in God, or agnostic, or atheist.

The documents treated come from a period of nearly a hundred years, a period which was born in the rough wake of the first industrial revolution and has seen us, its people, engineer further acceleration of change. Now consider the dates of the documents: 1891, 1931, 1961, 1963, 1965, 1965 again, 1967, five more in the 1970's and eight in the 1980's. The Church's teaching responds to the acceleration.

Eight documents in the eighties. If this book also covered the two Instructions on Liberation, approved by Pope John Paul II and issued by the Congregation for the Doctrine of the Faith, the figure for the eighties would rise to ten.[8] The Instruction of 1984 considers theologies (some though not all akin to Marxism) conceived in the struggles to remedy the economic and other wrongs that afflict Latin America. The paper of 1986, after reviewing Western ideas of freedom, from Renaissance to twentieth century, suggests the main elements of Christian doctrine on freedom and liberation.

There can be few subjects more important than freedom, in Britain no less than for Latin America. An understanding of the full meaning of freedom is important too, and the Vatican Instructions contain much to consider. They cannot however be appropriately summarized within the size of the present work.

In December 1988 – to complete the tally, to date of writing – the Vatican's Congregation for Catholic Education, in co-operation with the Council for Justice and Peace, produced *Guidelines for the Study and Teaching of the Church's Social Doctrine*, a 90-page survey of the whole doctrine, for bishops and teachers.[9] The present work has a different perspective.

The individual

As this book reaches each document, it gives chief attention to teachings pertinent to the role of the individual, in economic life: the individual alone, and together with others. Save as helpful or necessary, attention is not given to other facets of life, such as marriage, culture, and politics, nor to the roles of

Authority or State, nor to the international scene. Throughout, the country particularly in mind is Britain.

The social doctrine in full considers many facets of life, and every sphere from that of the individual alone to the summits of national and international authority. The spheres can be seen as five: individual; family; then the sphere the Church sometimes calls intermediary, between individual and family on the one hand and the State on the other; the State; the international scene.

The Church sees an especial importance for us in the third sphere, at society's centres where we work together in association more or less freely chosen: our enterprises commercial and social, private cooperative and public, local and national, charitable, cultural, educational, artistic, professional, political, and sporting; our fellowships, movements, societies, and trusts; our human networks (new members of this company and its vocabulary). In the economy, businesses and trade unions are prominent in this sphere. And in Britain, where we do not like our doctrine joyless, we have clubs and pubs.

Paragraphs 59 to 67 of Pope John's *Mater et Magistra*[10] are among the many of the social teaching which see this special importance. The understanding finds expression also in emphasis upon rights of Association, Enterprise and Economic Initiative, on "Intermediary Bodies" and Social Growth, and on the Common Good, Community and Society. Reference to the terms in the Index will confirm.

It is perhaps a pity that the social doctrine uses the word "intermediary", suggesting something that's neither one thing nor the other, subservient to more important forces on either side. "Central" might be better. The third sphere is in fact central among the five. (Some of the social doctrine's translators from Latin have attempted to saddle this central and attractive field of human life with a second unattractive word, worse than "intermediary" – to wit, "socialization". See page 49-50 below.)

So this book gives attention to economic life in the first three spheres: individual, family, and centre. It also gives attention to the Church's teaching for the everyday: our everyday life and work at home, in the family, and in family business, for example; alone or with colleagues beyond the family, in production, service or supply of small, medium, or large scale, in enterprise private, cooperative, or public, whether we are our own boss or are partner, employee, contractor, trade-unionist, manager, director, entrepreneur, owner, shareholder or anything else, whether we work on land or sea or under or above them, and whatever our calling, trade or profession. It presents teaching on our ownership of home, business and other property, and on our use of these assets for the benefit of ourself and of others; on our producing, demanding and consuming; on our pay and profit, our spending and investing. The economy, after all, is not entirely made by governments, by other people, by Them. It is also made by Us.

Thirdly, this book has an eye for a further emphasis in the Church's teaching: the need for education and training, professional and technical, social and moral.

Thus, the portion of the social doctrine this book offers is substantial, though not the full meal. There are only tastes of the food-for-thought the Church offers on the responsibilities of the State.

Space is a reason for the omissions. There is also a reason for the choice of what not to omit, for the attention to the first three spheres and the economic everyday; namely that this is where we ourselves, writer and reader, can join Christ's Church in recognizing the importance of economic activity and the benefits it can offer humankind, and where we can respond to her calls for truly better achievement and for standards that are more human.

"Why don't They do something about it?" "The Government really should..." How often words like these are in our minds, and on our tongues! "The Government" so very often – whatever its colour.

"They" do indeed have responsibilities, as the Church reminds them. But the Church also reminds Us – first and foremost those of us who are her own members – that alone and with others We have opportunities and responsibilities, in our economically significant activities as in other departments of our lives: We – the writer and the reader; each and every one of us as an individual; and in our families; and in our work with others.

The Church's reminders are repeated many times, as the

pages following this Introduction witness. The opening pages of the summaries from Pope John's *Mater et Magistra* provide examples. Paragraphs 38, 43 and 67 of the Second Vatican Council's *Gaudium et Spes* see the everyday as a workshop powered by Christ's own example, and by the most vital force human beings possess.[11]

As long ago as 1931, Pius XI reminded us that whilst the State has important responsibilities, it is wrong for the State to take on too much: he affirmed the principle of subsidiary function, or Subsidiarity.[12] (The terms are believed to be derived from the Latin *subsidium:* assistance, help, support, protection – a meaning akin to a prime meaning of "subsidiary" in English. In the social doctrine the terms do not carry the other meaning sometimes used in English, viz. minor, subordinate.)

In 1946 Pius XII reaffirmed the principle.[13] In 1949, speaking to businessmen, he stated a similar rule: "It is the task of public right to serve private right and not to absorb it. No more than any other branch of human activity is the economy of its nature an institution of the State. On the contrary, it is the living product of the free initiative of individuals and of the groups they freely form."[14]

Reminders are repeated by Pope John XXIII, by the Second Vatican Council, and by Popes Paul VI and John Paul II, with emphasis on association, for achieving what lone individuals cannot.[15]

Solidarity and Subsidiarity

To the need and right for individuals to associate, the Church adds a further emphasis: the need for a new Solidarity. What we may dub The Two S's are brought together in 1986 by the Vatican's Congregation for the Doctrine of the Faith in the second of the Instructions already referred to:

"Linked to human dignity are the principle of Solidarity and the principle of Subsidiarity.

"By virtue of the first, man with his brothers is obliged to contribute to the common good of society at all its levels. Hence the Church's doctrine is opposed to all forms of social or political individualism.

"By virtue of the second, neither the State nor any society must ever substitute itself for the initiative and responsibility of individuals and of intermediate communities at the level on which they can function, nor must they take away the room necessary for their freedom. Hence the Church's social doctrine is opposed to all forms of collectivism...

"The Church is of course aware of the complexity of the problems confronting society and of the difficulties in finding solutions. Nevertheless she considers that the first thing to be done is to appeal to the spiritual and moral capacities of the individual and to the permanent need for inner conversion, if one is to achieve the economic and social changes that will truly be at the service of man..."[16]

Solidarity and Subsidiarity are again treated together, in 1988, by the Congregation for Catholic Education in their *Guidelines*.[17]

It is not always easy to see the connections between our ordinary daily life and job, Christ's example, and the fight against hunger, injustice and need. It is not always easy to see opportunities within our own spheres one, two and three and our own economic everyday, to help build a better world.

Despite our complaints about "Them", there is at least a part of us which recognises that the world is not, really, entirely made by "Them"; but when we seek ourselves to work for a better world, we seem sometimes to imagine that all the needs and opportunities lie outside our own economic everyday. We respond to appeals for money and we raise money, for charities and for just causes. After our normal working day or week is over, we give our labour and time to charities and just causes. We personally help and serve people in need.

In face of injustice and need at home and abroad, response of kinds such as these can be clamantly necessary; can indeed be Christlike. The Church calls for response to injustice and need, and has always called for it. From her heart she thanks and commends those who give themselves in ways such as these. *But the Church has always also called us and in her social doctrine calls us now to build the better world within our own everyday*. If we find it difficult to see how we can respond to the everyday call, here is perhaps a further reason for the attention given it in this book.

Competence

Consider for a moment one of the down-to-earth words of the social doctrine: *Competence. Peritia* in Latin: competence, expertise, proficiency, skill, in English translations. In documents also concerned with what we might think of as loftier things, the Second Vatican Council, popes and bishops all consider it right to mention the value of competence. The Council calls for this capability in one of the most forceful paragraphs of *Gaudium et Spes*, one of the few paragraphs from the Council with severity in it. Echoing Pope John XXIII,[18] the words condemn the notion that the Christian can shirk earthly responsibility, remember Christ's threat of punishment and the example of Christ's working life as carpenter, and invite a striving for competence.[19]

Linked with the calls for competence are repeated appeals to educate and train. Linked also are reminders that greater skill in the use of human capability and earthly resource can quicken our response to hunger and poverty. Other paragraphs of the social teaching make it clear that the competence we learn must be professional and technical, and more: we must become skilled in the human and moral dimensions of economic life, as well as the professional and technical.[20]

Consider these teachings in relation to our economic everyday in Britain. Suppose our work is in industry, business or service, or in agriculture or deep-sea fishing – in some part of the food business, for example. Suppose that as individuals in this business, and in our families, in our education and training, in the associations and unions we belong to and in the enterprises where we work, we give more time and resource to the cultivation of competence.

Next suppose that we succeed in enhancing our skill in finding ways of satisfying the needs of customers and potential customers. Suppose in particular that we enhance our skill in finding ways of satisfying needs less expensively – through more skilful methods for instance, and not solely by cutting human labour, for unemployment.

Now couple these possibilities with teachings such as the Common Good,[21] with the wrongs of excessive consumption, and with the Church's appeals for those in need. If in our food business we have in the past sometimes shared a habit of seeking maximum reward for the improvements we make, suppose we moderate the habit just a little. Suppose we take to ourself in higher profit and higher pay just a little less of the saving we have achieved through more skilful methods. Suppose finally that we pass more of the saving to the customer than was our habit, in lower prices, or at least in lesser price increases.

Lower prices or lesser price increases could enable customers to buy who now cannot afford to buy at all, or who cannot afford enough for their needs. Not all customers and potential customers in Britain, on the Continent and overseas are rich. And might the additional purchases help sustain British employment?

Is the church's teaching for the economic everyday perhaps in some kind of touch with realistic possibilities, after all? Is it perhaps in true touch with the world's needs, and with our own?

Before turning to the last section of this Introduction, it is as well to register three points:

First, the Church's recognition of individual responsibility is no kind of approval of that exaggeration known as individual*ism*. The nature of the human being, social as well as individual; the achievements we enjoy through social growth; our share in responsibility for the common good; justice and love for our neighbour, especially our neighbour in need: these and other teachings make the Church's view clear. The social doctrine expressly disapproves individualism.

Second, the author has no ideological or political intent. Whether the Church's teaching has ideological or political implications and if so whether they tell for Left, Right or Centre are questions for the reader.

Third, though the State receives scant attention in this book, the Church sees important responsibilities for the State and for public institutions, as well as for individuals. She addresses much of her teaching to Authority, at all levels, national and international; and to her own leaders. She emphasizes in particular that in the interests of the disadvantaged, the poor, the weak and all in need, far and near, there are responsibilities of especial importance which belong to Authority as well as to

Us. She also encourages us to use our vote, and to participate in political life.

It can be rewarding to study the Church's economic and social doctrine in full. Go first to the Second Vatican Council's *Gaudium et Spes*.[22] Fruit of three years' work by bishops, advisers and popes in the light of Christian understanding, this Constitution examines humanity's situation in the world, our human nature and concerns, the roles of individuals alone and together, and the roles of Church and State.

Responsibility, justice and love

An early paragraph of this Introduction referred to key principles. Responsibility is one of them. The words "responsible" and "responsibility" recur again and again in the social doctrine. They connote the capability, dignity and vocation of every human being, as well as duty. Justice is another prominent theme. The powerful meanings in these words, in the social teaching, are similar to their meanings in ordinary language, though Jesus' Church sees in them rather more for us and for herself than is comfortable.

The third key word is the most important. It too is used in ordinary language, and in language not so ordinary. It carries a range of meanings. In the social doctrine, however, and in all Christian teaching, the third word has the most powerful of any meaning we can know in our lives, for the third word is love.

"Which is the first of all the Commandments?" asked one of the scribes, learned in the Law of Moses. Jesus replied, "This is the first:... You must love the Lord your God with all your heart, with all your soul, with all your mind and with all your strength. The second is this: You must love your neighbour as yourself..."[23] Later, at the Last Supper with his disciples, the evening before his trial, condemnation and death, Jesus said: "I give you a new commandment: love one another; you must love one another *just as I have loved you*".[24] The words in italics indicate the new element in the old command.

The Church's social doctrine confirms the teaching, for us now, two thousand years later, in a world in some ways so different from the Middle East of the scribes and the first disciples. "The fundamental law of human perfection and hence of the transformation of the world is the new commandment of love... The way of love is open to everyone... This love is not something reserved for important matters, but must be exercised above all in the ordinary circumstances of daily life."[25] Pope John XXIII calls love the "driving force" of the social doctrine.[26]

Love of God and neighbour, as Jesus Christ loved, two thousand years ago – in our daily life in Britain, today? In our daily work at home and in the family? In our work for pay or profit, beyond home and family? In our work with colleagues, and for customers? In our business life? In our trade union life? In our spending, home-owning and investing?

If we find the suggestions difficult, even bizarre or laughable, a reason may be that we have an inadequate understanding of how Jesus Christ loved; an inadequate understanding of the human characteristics or qualities of his love.

Some of us may think of love as meaning primarily qualities such as compassion, kindness, sympathy, readiness to help others, readiness to relieve disability and suffering, generosity, warm-heartedness – qualities which can be called virtues of the heart. Jesus is a magnificent example of these virtues; and he warns that God judges us according to our practice of them or our neglect.[27]

But Jesus' example of love is not limited to the virtues of the heart alone. It is not limited to the compassion he showed in his healing of the disabled, the diseased and the troubled – compassion and power marvellous enough without more, one might think. Consider some of the further aspects of Jesus' life, and the further human qualities they reveal. (In Christ's life, in supreme degree, there are also the super-human qualities, as in some degree there can be in every life: faith, for example; communion with God the Father. What follows here, however, confines itself to the human.)

As a human being, Christ was a village carpenter who in his thirties took on the job of teaching and saving his nation, and foreigners too if they believed in him. The need of these peoples for God's guidance was profound, as in differing ways the need of every human people always is. Their need also had the acutenesses of its particular time and facts. Jesus left his village of Nazareth, proclaimed his message, recruited a team, and began his mission.

In town and country, in public and in private, Christ spoke perceptively and with learning, authority, and Jewish wit, to thousands of people in all walks of life. In word and deed he revealed God's nature and programme, and indicated what the response of individual and nation should be. He exposed falsity, pretence, and abuse of power. He became known throughout the land, and in its capital, Jerusalem.

Meeting some readiness to understand, and much resistance, Jesus persevered, with gentleness and with firmness. He continued to train, guide and encourage his team. He entrusted them with a share in his work, and with responsibility for carrying it on after his death. (The Gospels must be studied in order to begin to appreciate the size of job Christ took on, its practical and other difficulties, and the way Christ carried it through. Accounts of the political, religious and socio-economic situations in which Jesus worked can further assist understanding.[28])

The authorities became increasingly hostile. Christ saw that his mission was going to land him in rejection and death. Yet he sustained his campaign for two years or more. He progressively stepped it up. He rode into the capital, acted and spoke there in ways almost bound to lead to arrest and condemnation, and suffered the consequences.

All this Jesus did for the benefit of others, for he saw that his mission, suffering, death and resurrection, and the unkillable love at work throughout and always, would offer eternal salvation to his own and to all nations, of his time and of all times.

Heart and head: instruments of love

Consider then some of the human qualities of Jesus' love, shown in his undertaking that mission and carrying it through: concern for truth, concern for knowledge of the true causes of troubles, readiness to share knowledge; forethought, grasp of priorities and practicalities, judgement; boldness, firmness, perceptiveness, wit, perseverance, courage; commitment; the will to give oneself in service; willingness to work with and through others, and to help others develop their capabilities; willingness to share power – qualities which can be called virtues of the head as well as the heart.

If some of us have tended to think that love can use only virtues of the heart, a few seconds' reflection must remind us that love can use virtues of the head as well – the strengths of mind and will which God shared in unique measure with his Son and which in some measure he offers to every one of us. Take marriage as a first example. Every husband, every wife, knows that the head can assist, as well as the heart, in making a good marriage: forethought, perceptivity, commitment, willingness to share.

Heart and head, both, can be instruments of love in our work too, whether we work in the family and at home, or in business or otherwise outside. We can use mind and will as instruments of love in economic matters of any of the kinds instanced in this Introduction. Concern for knowledge of the true causes of troubles, readiness to share knowledge and power; the will to serve – to serve family, and colleagues at work; the will to serve the needs of customers, rich and poor; forethought, commitment, grasp of priorities and practicalities; willingness to work with and through others, and to help others develop their capabilities; good judgement, boldness, firmness, perceptivity; wit... Everyone who works at home or outside, everyone in business, know that qualities like these can help make an enterprise alive with effectiveness and humanness. Qualities like these can empower and humanize an economy.

The Church's recognition that love can guide our daily work is close to her reminders that in our daily work we can partner God himself. God's is a work of love. If in partnership with him, so is ours.[29]

So the love the Church speaks of is Christlike self-giving love. It includes commitment, service and sacrifice. It is not just affection, feeling, emotion or passion. It is more than even compassion, alone.

Unpalatable as it may sometimes be for those of us who in material things are relatively well-off, Christ's Church teaches that an especially insistent call of this love is a call to solidarity, a call to help people far and near to lift themselves out of hunger, poverty, disease, and situations that are dead-ends to development and human fulfilment for themselves and their children.[30]

Christian love is however more than emergency aid and fund-raising. It is more than social work private and public, more than paid and unpaid work by and for charities – Christlike though all such action can be. "Certainly this love is expressed in many kinds of voluntary work... But it is expressed in an equally challenging way in the quest for justice through *economic*, juridical, social, political and cultural initiatives. True charity is not exhausted in what are called charitable activities, but is the guide and stimulus for every work of justice and fellowship," Pope John Paul II said in 1988.[31] (In 1989 John Paul II pointed out that head is needed as well as heart, in work of the kind traditionally first thought of as charitable no less than in initiatives of newer kinds: "Through her charitable or socio-charitable organizations in all countries the Church strives to assist the distressed with the respect and tenderness of her divine Founder, but also with *the human qualities of perspicacity and objectivity, method and perseverance* ".[32])

"Human work in the production and exchange of goods or in the provision of services surpasses all other elements of economic life," the Second Vatican Council affirms, and goes on to remind us that by our ordinary daily work we not only provide for self and family and serve our fellows: we can also "*exercise genuine charity* and be a partner in the work of bringing divine creation to perfection".[33] In our work we can "exercise charity to the full": an alternative translation.[34] (In Christian speech and writing "charity" normally means the same as the Christian love considered in these pages, though "charity" can more precisely mean the divine or supernatural virtue which fires it.)

This love, breath of God himself, is not something high-flown, "reserved for important matters", nor is it just for exceptional people: it is exercised "above all in the ordinary circumstances of daily life", and it is a way "open to everyone".[35] "Let no-one imagine that a life of activity in the world is incompatible with spiritual perfection. The two can very well be harmonized. It is a gross error to suppose that we cannot perfect ourselves except by putting aside all worldly activity..."[36] "Let Christians follow the example of Christ, who worked as a craftsman. Let them be proud of the opportunity to carry out their earthly activity in such a way as to integrate human, domestic, professional, scientific and technical enterprises with religious values..."[37]

Men and women throughout Britain know that self-giving love is for everyday life and work. Often readily, sometimes after a tussle with themselves, they live up to commitment and they give generous, thoughtful service, at home and in business; often at personal sacrifice. Without fuss, without trumpeting, they allow love to guide them, even though many might be embarrassed or reluctant to use the word. For any, however, who find the concept of everyday love difficult, especially perhaps love in economic activity, it may be helpful to consider a little further the part of Christ's life referred to in the passage last quoted above – Christ's work as craftsman, work closer to what many of us do today than the public mission of Christ's later years.

The workshop of Joseph and Jesus

Jesus was in his thirties when he left Nazareth and began his public work. So from an age – say, sixteen or seventeen? – at which in a Galilean village a son probably began to give substantial assistance to a working father (in Jesus' case his foster-father, Joseph) Jesus had fifteen to twenty years of youth and adulthood before he left. The public work, by contrast, lasted three or four years at most, from outset to crucifixion.

The Gospels record that Joseph and Jesus were carpenters, and it seems that Jesus worked as a carpenter for most or all of the Nazareth years. "Jesus devoted most of the years of his life on earth to manual work at the carpenter's bench."[38]

The Gospels also indicate that Joseph, Mary and Jesus were not well-off. Almost certainly, the carpentry had to earn money, or money's worth.

At first, Jesus probably assisted Joseph. Later, if the foster-father had died before the younger man began his public mission (as it seems Joseph had) Jesus may have run the business.

A romantic notion of the work Joseph and Jesus did would probably be mistaken. There was first the need to earn a livelihood. Then there were the work's demands. Equipment and tools for agriculture, construction and transport, for example, which today come mainly in metals, from factories, made greater use of wood in Christ's time. Much of all this came from the carpenter. The work was probably sometimes heavy, as well as skilled. Customers' needs must often have been pressing (perhaps sometimes the competition, too?).

Now Jesus Christ was and is himself love, in the fullest sense. On earth he was love in human flesh and blood. He was and is the Son of God. If money-earning daily work for customers could not be done with love, and in partnership with God, Christ would never have touched it.

That glimpse is all the Bible gives us of Christ's ordinary working life. Christ, however, founded a community, his Church, and promised that the Holy Spirit would teach it everything and lead it to the complete truth.[39] The teaching for ordinary working life which this Church passes on to us is abundant.

The Church considers first what we put into daily work. She speaks of our input, to use a current word: competence, honesty, service, fulfilment of fair contracts.[40] She emphasizes enterprise, initiative, participation, responsibility: characteristics which lift service out of servility. She warmly commends progress in science and technology, provided we do not worship it.

The Church suggests next the spirit in which we can take out of our work. She speaks of our out-take: pay and profit, both, but not necessarily and always the maximum; pay and profit considerate of prices, and of the interests of customers rich and poor; pay and profit considerate of those outside the business as well as those within it. She reminds us that our lifestyle can reflect something of the Sermon on the Mount, moderating our need and appetite for ever-increasing gains.

Thirdly, the Church speaks of the purposes underlying her suggestions. She speaks of the self-development and fulfilment we can enjoy through work and service; of partnership with God in his continuing creation of the world; of justice, solidarity, and the common good; of the rights and the obligations of ownership. She reminds us that God has destined the earth's resources and goods for all human beings far and near, to be shared fairly; that excessive disparities militate against human dignity, and against peace; that there is need for a preference for the poor – above all, for those without hope of a better future for themselves and their children.

The Church presents her teaching in the name of Jesus Christ who is love. She reminds us that despite all fault and difficulty, the Holy Spirit offers help to every man and woman of goodwill, believer or not, who is trying to lead a life in tune with her teaching.[41]

Countless men and women do lead lives in tune with the Church's teaching. We readily recognize this when their work is person-to-person and its goodness is plain. We recognize it in service paid and unpaid, at home and outside. We recognize the life of a committed good husband, wife, parent, school-teacher. We recognize the work of our men and women in the ambulance, fire, lifeboat and police services when they save life, and the work of our nurses, nuns, doctors and surgeons who heal the sick and care for the injured, the infirm and the dying.

We may also recognize – even in our modern world of businesses bigger than the workshop of Joseph and Jesus – the work of someone in business, who is not only good at his or her job but is also understanding, helpful and reliable to colleagues. We are perhaps not so ready to recognize service to people the worker is not in immediate contact with.

Farmer; skipper and crew of a deep-sea trawler; technician manager or director in a food processing plant; stock controller at a food wholesaler's; worker in agricultural or marine research – these and their like meet and know few of the people they help to feed at home and abroad. The man or woman whose job is in vehicle manufacture has personal contact with few of the people who drive the cars or trucks he or she helps to make. When we turn on a tap and draw water from mains and reservoirs, when we flush waste away down to the sewers, we are nearly always unknown to the men and women who ensure that these systems are laid, cleaned and kept up.

Yet every man and woman in food, cars, trucks or water (these are but examples of course) who puts his or her best into the business, contributing qualities such as those exemplified by Jesus and commended by his Church, who takes pay and profit out of the business in the measure and spirit commended by Jesus and his Church, and who lives and works like this to benefit others as well as self – every such person lives and works in tune with the teaching summarized in this book. Every such person fulfils in the economy Jesus' commandment of love.

NOTES
[Page numbers refer to pages in this book]

[1]John XXIII, 1961: *Mater et Magistra* §222, 223 (page 58). See also Paul VI, *Octogesima Adveniens* §4 (page 107).

[2]Vatican II, 1965: *Apostolicam Actuositatem* §§31, 32 (page 86).

[3]Bishops' Conference of England and Wales, 1980: *The Easter People* §162 (page 125). See also *Christifideles Laici*, 1988 §60 (page 181).

[4]Nature of Doctrine: *Sollicitudo Rei Socialis* §41, (page 170). See also Note 9 below, and Index, Social Doctrine.

[5]Congregation for Catholic Education, 1988: *Guidelines* §1 (see Annex 2).

[6]*Mater et Magistra* §221.

[7]*Gaudium et Spes* §§2, 3 (not summarized in the present work).

[8]*Theology of Liberation* (1984, 33 pages) and *Christian Freedom and Liberation* (1986, 56 pages): see Annex 2.

[9]*Guidelines*, 1988: see Annex 2. *Guidelines* reviews the nature, history, principles, criteria and directives of the social doctrine.

[10]*Mater et Magistra* §§59-67 (pages 52-53).

[11]*Gaudium et Spes* §§38, 43, 67 (pages 73, 73-74, 76). The everyday a workshop: see also pages 28-30.

[12]Subsidiarity: *Quadragesimo Anno* §§78-80 (page 45).

[13]Pius XII, 1946: quoted by Calvez in *L'Économie, L'Homme, La Société*, p.45 (Annex 2).

[14]Pius XII, 1949: quoted by Kirwan on p.63 of his study-edition of *Rerum Novarum* (see Annex 2). *Acta Apostolicae Sedis* 1949, p. 285.

[15]Reminders: *Mater et Magistra* (§§51-55, 65-67,117, 152 in particular, in the full text) *Pacem in Terris* §24, page 63; *Gaudium et Spes* §§34-43 and 65-75 (pages 72-74, 76-79); *Populorum Progressio* §33 (page 92); *Laborem Exercens* §82-83 (page 141).

[16]The Two S's: *Christian Freedom and Liberation*, Chapter V, from §§73 and 75.

[17]The Two S's: *Guidelines for the Study and Teaching of Social Doctrine*, §38.

[18]John XXIII: e.g. *Mater et Magistra* §255 (page 53).

[19]*Competence, Gaudium et Spes*: §43 (pages 73-74). See also Index.

[20]See also Index references under e.g. Education, Human Being, Morality, Science and Technology.

[21]*Common Good*: consider for example Pope John XXIII's teaching in §§78-81 of *Mater et Magistra* (page 54).

[22]*Gaudium et Spes*: for publishers etc. of full texts, see Annex 2. Part-summarized in this book from page 70.

[23]The Great Commandments: Mark 12:28-31 (Annex 1).

[24]The New Commandment: John 13:31, 34-35 (Annex 1).

[25]*Gaudium et Spes* §38, (page 73).

[26]*Mater et Magistra* §226 (page 58).

[27]The Last Judgement: Matthew 25:31-46 (Annex 1).

[28]Accounts can be found in Bible commentaries (see Annex 2, page 192).

[29]Partnership with God: *Mater et Magistra* §§254-256 and 259 (page 53); *Gaudium et Spes* §§34, 57, 67 (pages 72, 75, 76); *Populorum Progressio* §27 (page 91); *Laborem Exercens* §§113-118 (page 145).

[30]Dead-ends: see e.g. *Gaudium et Spes*, *Populorum Progressio* and *Sollicitudo Rei Socialis* (pages 70-72, 93-94 and 170).

[31]John Paul II, Address to men and women working at all levels in agriculture, industry and trade, assembled at the Ferrari motor works at Fiorano, *L'Osservatore Romano*, 1 August 1988.

[32]John Paul II, *L'Osservatore Romano*, 21 August 1989.

[33]Love in work: *Gaudium et Spes* §67 (page 76).

[34]Translation by William Purdy, CTS Do363 (see Annex 2).

[35]*Gaudium et Spes* §38 (page 73).

[36]*Mater et Magistra* §255 (page 53).

[37]*Gaudium et Spes* §43 (page 73). See also *Laborem Exercens* §§26, 113-118 (pages 135, 145).

[38]*Laborem Exercens* §§26, 118 (pages 135, 145). John Paul II devotes the whole of this encyclical to the question of work.

[39] Holy Spirit: John 14:26; 16:12-13.

[40]For sources of the teachings referred to here and in the paragraphs that follow, see the Index.

[41]Holy Spirit: *Gaudium et Spes* §§22, 38 (pages 70, 73); *Christifideles Laici* §§16 and 17 (page 176).

RERUM NOVARUM

The Condition of the Working Classes

1891

Encyclical Letter of Pope Leo XIII

Most papal documents are named and known by the Latin of their first words. So it is with Pope Leo XIII's encyclical.

In the context, *Rerum Novarum* means "of revolutionary change". The English subtitle *The Condition of the Working Classes* translates a description of the document's subject given by Pope Leo XIII on his opening page. *Rerum Novarum* is also sometimes called "The Workers' Charter".

Revolutionary change it was, that led to this encyclical: the industrial revolution, economic and social change; scientific discovery, commercial expansion, new wealth, new power – and, disfiguring these advances, new exploitation and injustice for many. Revolutionary change has continued and has even accelerated, accompanied by a growing volume of reflection, reminder and suggestion from the Church.

Rerum Novarum begins the book of the Church's modern social teaching. The encyclical is not in the book merely as an historical curio: it is the book's first chapter, affirmed and reaffirmed, as well as developed, in later pages. Popes of the twentieth century refer to *Rerum Novarum* again and again.

Let us look at some of the matters Pope Leo XIII considers. First, the matter of property and ownership.

Misuse of ownership and power by second-rate business people is probably ceaseless. In the nineteenth century it was ceaseless and gross.

Though there were shining exceptions, many factory-owners, employers and shareholders kept for themselves all ownership, control and decision, maximum profit, and the entire capital appreciation from growth. Some treated employees like subhumans. They paid subminimum wages. They used even children for long days of hard labour at a halfpenny an hour. They did nothing to help educate their workers or to develop employees' capabilities. Many workers and their families laboured in near-slavery and lived in squalor.

Reacting against this, Marxists and others campaigned for transfer of ownership to the State: ownership of the means of production, in particular. The State would decide the use of its assets, for the good of all. In some countries the transfer was made.

This is a reason why in his encyclical Pope Leo XIII considered private ownership of property first. Far from commending its abolition, the Pope understood that private ownership is a human right, and that it includes but is not limited to ownership of businesses. He also saw that in addition to the matter of ownership, there is the matter of use: our use of earthly assets should be in accord with justice and love. The assets are not evil. Misuse is the evil.

As the reader will see from the documents following Leo XIII's encyclical, the twentieth century Church both maintains and develops this teaching. She maintains it for the many who still ow . less than their fair share. And for the growing number of us who, compared with our poor at home and abroad, are now becoming rich in property and in capability, she stresses more and more our responsibility to use our assets for the benefit of others as well as self.[1]

For us British there is continuing pertinence in other teachings of Pope Leo XIII, too: in the duties of employers and employees, for example, and in the recognition of trade union membership as a further human right. The Church's teaching on justice between employer and employee, with regard to pay in particular, was much debated in the wake of *Rerum Novarum*. This teaching has since been developed.[2] There are useful notes on this in Joseph Kirwan's study-edition of the encyclical.[3]

Parts of Leo XIII's paragraph 42 may seem quaint to some British trade unionists. As the Church teaches, however, religion and morality concern our role in the economy no less than in other parts of our lives. There is nothing inappropriate in the duties seen in paragraph 42.

In the two final sections summarized below, Pope Leo gives us two of the chief Christian teachings: teachings well-founded and wise, however difficult we sometimes find it to liv ~ them.

RERUM NOVARUM

Private property

§§4-12 (35).   It is the right of every human being to have ownership of private property, for self and for family. "Every man has by nature the right to possess property as his own." A worker has the right to own and manage earnings and savings, and property bought with them: possessions for example; land built on or cultivated; investments for income; and property to pass to the children.[4]

§8.   Private ownership is in conformity with human nature; it is in accord with natural law. Divine law adds its sanction, forbidding us even to covet what belongs to someone else.[5]

§§9-10.   The right to property belongs to individuals and to heads of families; indeed "that right is all the stronger in proportion as the human person receives a wider extension in the family". Provision for the family's future requires ownership of productive property[6] which can be left to the children as inheritance.

§§10, 12, 30, 35.   The State must uphold and favour the right of private ownership. "Policy should be to induce as many as possible of the people to become owners." First among good results will be a more equitable distribution of property.

Use of our assets

§§18-19.   Good, generous use of our property, for the benefit of others as well as self, is crucial. The amount of it is not. In particular, we who have abundance of blessings – whether material goods, or gifts of the mind – must use them to perfect our own nature and also to help those who are poor or in need. We must share them with those who are poor or in need.[7] We should tremble at Christ's warnings that if we are selfish we risk eternal loss and punishment.[8] We will have to give a most strict account to the Supreme Judge for all we possess.[9]

Capital and labour

§§15.   The notion that class is naturally hostile to class is false
and irrational. Capital cannot do without labour, nor labour
without capital.

Employment and pay

§§15-17, 33-34.   Among our duties as workers: fully and
faithfully to perform work which has been freely and equitably agreed; never to resort to violence. Among our duties as
owners and employers: not to misuse or overwork men and
women as if they were slaves, or just things or tools for gain,
but to respect their human dignity and worth and their needs
material and spiritual; to harmonize the demands of work with
our employees' age and health, and with their need for rest; to
respect the special competences and the family needs of women;
not to employ children in any way harmful to their growth or
education.
    In particular it is the duty of owners and employers to pay
remuneration that is just, and sufficient for human livelihood,
never trying to claw back. To pay less whilst making a profit
is wicked injustice, even supposing the contract to have been
freely entered into.[10]

The social action of the Church[11]

§22.   "The Church does her utmost to teach, to train, to
educate... to influence mind and heart so that all may willingly
yield themselves to be formed and guided by the commandments of God. It is in this fundamental matter that the Church
possesses a power peculiarly her own. The agencies she employs
are given her by Jesus Christ himself for the very purpose of
reaching the hearts of men and women... They alone can reach
the innermost heart and conscience, and bring men and women
to act from a motive of duty, to control their passions and
appetites, to love God and their neighbours with a love that is
outstanding and of the highest degree..."

The Church not concerned with the soul alone[11]

§23. "Neither must it be supposed that the solicitude of the Church is so preoccupied with spiritual concerns as to neglect temporal and earthly interests. Her desire is that the poor, for example, should rise above poverty and wretchedness...

"Christian morality, when adequately and completely practised, leads of itself to temporal prosperity,[12] for it merits the blessing of that God who is the source of all blessings; it restrains the greed of possession...; it teaches contentment with a frugal standard of living..."[13]

Trade unions and other associations

§§36-38, 41, 43. As employers and as employees we can do much through associations and organizations. Examples are societies for mutual help; benevolent foundations for cases of accident, sickness and death; institutions for the welfare of children and young people, and of adults; organizations for bettering the position of workers, for developing skills and for fostering employment. The most important of all these are trade unions suited to the requirements of the age.

"To enter into a society of this kind is the natural right of man." The State must protect such rights, without heavy-handed intrusion into the associations' internal affairs.

§42. We should organize and run our trade unions so that in the best way they help each individual member to better his or her situation to the utmost in body, soul and property. We should give special and chief attention to religion and morality, and should accord to religious instruction the foremost place.

Sundays

§§16, 32-33, 42. We should stop work on Sundays and holy days, for rest and refreshment, to forget business, and to worship God. As owners and employers and as trade unionists we should foster and facilitate this.

The key

§45.   The key to success in all these matters is self-giving love.[14]

NOTES

[Page numbers refer to pages in this book]

[1]See for example *Mater et Magistra* §§109-121 (page 56); *Gaudium et Spes* §§26-32 and 69-71 (pages 71-72, 78); *Homeless* II 3, III 2-4, IV 1 (pages 162-164); *Sollicitudo Rei Socialis* §42 (page 170).

[2]See for example *Quadragesimo Anno* §§53-75 (pages 44-45); *Laborem Exercens* §§88-90 (page 142).

[3]See pp. 35-65 in Kirwan: Annex 2 below.

[4]For further examples, see *Mater et Magistra* §§109-121, (page 56).

[5]Deuteronomy 5:21 from the Ten Commandments. See also Deuteronomy 5:19: "You must not steal".

[6]Productive property: "income-yielding property" in J. Kirwan's translation.

[7]We must share. "To share" can perhaps be considered a key verb in §§18-19 of *Rerum Novarum*. It occurs in two of the passages quoted by Leo XIII – "He that hath a talent", said St Gregory the Great, "let him see that he hide it not; he that hath abundance, let him quicken himself to mercy and generosity; he that hath art and skill, let him do his best *to share* the use and the utility thereof with his neighbour." "It is lawful" says St Thomas Aquinas, "for a man to hold private property; and it is also necessary for the carrying on of human existence." But if the question be asked, How must one's possessions be used?, the Church replies in the words of the same holy Doctor: "Man should not consider his material possessions as his own, but as common to all, so as *to share* them without hesitation when others are in need..." Kirwan translates Aquinas thus: "No man is entitled to manage things merely for himself, he must do so in the interests of all, so that he is ready *to share* with others in case of necessity..." On sharing, see also *Gaudium et Spes* §69.

[8]Matthew 19:23,24; Luke 6:24,25; Luke 16:19-31 (see Annex 1).

[9]Matthew 25:31-46: The Last Judgement (see Annex 1). See also the immediately preceding verses 14-30: the Parable of the Talents.

[10]*Rerum Novarum* as affirmed by Pope John XXIII in *Mater et Magistra* §18, and by Paul VI in *Populorum Progressio* §59.

[11]*The social action of the Church; The Church not concerned with the soul alone.* These subheads are taken from the 1960 edition of *Rerum Novarum* published by the Catholic Truth Society. Under these subheads, the present author quotes *verbatim* from the same edition. In the hundred years since Pope Leo XIII wrote the words of which those quoted are a translation, Catholic understanding of what "the Church" is has continued to grow, as the

reader will see from the more recent documents – for example: *Gaudium et Spes, Apostolicam Actuositatem,* the new *Code of Canon Law,* and *Christifideles Laici.* Perhaps more clearly than before, we now understand that the Church is not pope, bishops, priests, monks and nuns alone. The concern, the teaching, the action, the example of which Pope Leo XIII wrote in paragraphs 22 and 23 of *Rerum Novarum* are a responsibility which in some measure belongs to every Catholic – to every lay man and woman in ordinary daily life and work, as well as to the leaders and the solemnly consecrated. Perhaps we can read paragraphs 22 and 23 with this in mind.

[12]"Complete adherence to the code of Christian morals leads directly of itself to greater prosperity" (Kirwan's translation).

[13]"Contentment with a frugal standard of living": a contentment perhaps difficult for some of us twentieth-century Northerners to imagine? Substitute "simpler" or "less affluent" for "frugal", or "a standard of living less wasteful of earth's resources"; and leave the twentieth century for the twenty-first. This may bring us the idea?

[14]Self-giving love: see pages 24-32 above.

QUADRAGESIMO ANNO

The Social Order

1931

Encyclical Letter of Pope Pius XI

"Forty Years have elapsed since the incomparable Encyclical of Leo XIII...": thus Pius XI begins. Subsequent popes have followed Pius XI in issuing social encyclicals or other communications upon anniversaries of *Rerum Novarum.*[1] *The Social Order* translates a subtitle of Pius XI's own.

A principle that concerns individual and State, recalled by Pius XI and reaffirmed since by popes and Council, is the "principle of subsidiary function" or "Subsidiarity".[2] Other teachings from the fifty pages of this encyclical, summarized below, maintain and develop the papal concerns for the rights and duties of ownership and employment, and for principles to guide our lives in the economy.

The heading *Capital and labour* reproduces that used in the English edition of *Quadragesimo Anno* published by the Catholic Truth Society.[3] The unique significance and value of human work – whether manual, managerial or intellectual, industrial, agricultural, maritime, artistic or of any other kind – in contrast to lifeless tools or things used in human work, such as equipment or money, can be seen through all the centuries from the creation: through the Old Testament, in the life of Christ, and since. In the most recent times, since *Quadragesimo Anno*, recognition of this significance and value has grown even clearer.[4] Today, Pius XI would probably write his heading as *Labour and capital*.

Pius XI, today, might make a second change, in his paragraphs 80-87. In these paragraphs the Pope commends what we could call modern guilds. Since conflict between employer and employee was much in Pius XI's mind in 1931, he mentions these two only, when suggesting that the guilds would represent whole sectors of activity, and not just the interests of one "side". Today, businesses and economic and social enterprises of many kinds are run by husbands and wives, by associations, members of cooperatives, partners, owners, co-owners, the self-employed, shareholders and others who may be neither employers nor employees, or neither of these exclusively. Today Pius XI might commend guilds open to everyone working in each field, whatever the level or nature of participation.

The paragraphs summarized under the present author's heading *Competition, power, profit : justice and love*[5] decline to accept unlimited free competition, profit and wealth by all and any means, and other anti-human notions, as principles to guide economic life. A long paragraph 132 in the final group condensed under this heading, notes in its full text "that unquenchable thirst for riches and possessions, which has at all times impelled men to break the law of God and trample on the rights of their neighbour" and continues:

"The uncertainty of economic life and especially of the economic régime demands the keenest uninterrupted straining of energy on the part of those engaged. As a result, some have become so hardened against the stings of conscience as to hold all means good which enable them to increase their profits, and to safeguard against sudden changes of fortune the wealth amassed by great and assiduous efforts..."

The paragraph in full, and those that follow, express the Pope's concern at the seriously substandard behaviour of a minority in business – harmful profiteering and speculation, for example – and at behaviour as base as fraud or crime – such as fraudulent misuse or theft of investors' savings. No doubt we will always have these to fight.

May the Pope's words perhaps also have warning for the larger number of us who do not go so far as fraud or crime, but who do not always get our priorities right? "...the keenest uninterrupted straining of energy..."; profit increase before all else. Consider for example, some of us in business who handle clients' investments and who spend too much time with eyes rivetted to video displays of ever-changing prices, seeking short-term gain for client, for firm or for self, and too little time away from the office, with the men and women who are building our country's businesses big and small, learning of their work, their worth and longer-term potential, and of the investment they need.

QUADRAGESIMO ANNO

The Church's teaching

§§41-43.   Economics and morals are guided each by its own principles in its own sphere. The purpose of economics, however, is found in the individual and social nature of human beings and in God's design.

The same moral law which commands us to seek in our general conduct our supreme and final purpose in life, also commands us in every particular kind of activity to aim at the purpose which God has established for that order of activity, and to subordinate particular aims to our final purpose. So though it is not part of the Church's work to teach economic technique, it is part of her work to teach this moral law.[6]

Property

§§44-51 (61) (136).   Private ownership is both individual and social: a human right for self and family, and a means and obligation for serving society, for example by investing our savings so as to improve opportunity for productive work by others.

Capital and labour

§§53-65 (136).   "It is flagrantly unjust that capital or labour should deny the efficacy of the other, and claim all the profits." Each of us, employer or owner, and employee, should accord to the other a due share of the wealth to which he contributes, and a due share of social and economic progress.

In particular, for example where workers in industry or on the land still lack capital and property of their own, we should permit a just share only of the fruits of production to the wealthy, and pass an ample sufficiency to the workers. As employers and as owners,[7] we should do this primarily through payment of a just wage. When possible, however, job-contracts should also include elements of partnership, e.g. participation in ownership or management, or profit-sharing.

Employment and pay

§§69, 63-75 (110). Like ownership, employment is personal or individual, and also social. Unless intelligence, capital and labour combine for common effort, our work cannot produce its adequate fruits. If the social-individual character of labour be overlooked, we cannot justly value or reward it.

We must pay wages sufficient for earner and family. Mothers should not be forced to seek work outside the home, to the neglect of the children, because of insufficiency of the father's salary.

When agreeing pay, we must take the state of the business into account. It would be unjust to demand excessive wages which a business cannot pay without ruin, and harm to employment. On the other hand, difficulty from want of management energy or enterprise or from neglect of technical and economic progress is not a just reason for reducing wages.

Difficulty from outside the business, such as unjustly low prices, may raise different issues – in the last extreme, even the question whether the business can continue, or whether some other provision should be made for the employees. Employers and employed should join in plans and efforts to overcome difficulties and obstacles.

Finally, when agreeing pay we must consider the economic welfare of the community: for example, the paying of wages sufficient for savings and investment by employees; and the paying of wages at levels which foster employment rather than cause unemployment.

Subsidiarity[8]

§§78-80. Much that we cannot accomplish as individuals alone, we can best do by working together in association, rather than by looking to the State.

"Just as it is wrong to withdraw from the individual and commit to a group what private enterprise and industry can

accomplish, so too it is an injustice, a grave evil and a distur-
bance of right order, for a larger and higher association to
arrogate to itself functions that can be performed efficiently
by smaller and lower societies. This is a fundamental principle of social philosophy... Of its very nature the true aim of
all social activity should be to help members of the social
body, but never to destroy or absorb them."

"Directing, watching, stimulating, restraining, as circumstances suggest and necessity demands" – these are the tasks
for the State, tasks the State alone can effectively accomplish.

Modern guilds?

§§82-87.   We should consider the potential of self-governing associations, each open to everyone working in the same
trade, profession or field: open to employers and to employees. Such associations could promote the interests and the
standards of each sector, and could serve the common good.

Competition, power, profit: justice and love

§§56-61, 88, 97-98, 105-120, 130-137.   Free competition,
though within limits right and productive of good results, cannot
be the guiding principle of economic life. Nor can dictator-
ship, domination, or excessive economic or financial power,
public or private; nor mere individualism, profit and wealth
by all and any means, a lawless market, and survival of the
strongest; nor collectivist brands of atheism or materialism,
whether communist or socialist.

The guiding principles for our lives and work must be justice
and – above all – love, individual and social. Remembering
subsidiarity, Authority should foster a society inspired with
these principles, and should see that we keep our competition
and power within just limits.

We must reform our conduct, and give priority to the moral
rather than the material. Excessive concern for money or
possessions blocks growth of heart and mind.

NOTES
[Page numbers refer to pages in this book]

[1]Anniversaries: Broadcast by Pius XII, 1941 (pages 49, 59, note 4a), *Mater et Magistra* 1961, *Octogesima Adveniens* 1971, *Laborem Exercens* 1981.

[2]"Principle of subsidiary function" or "Subsidiarity": see *Quadragesimo Anno* §§78-80, *Mater et Magistra* §§ 51-67, and page 20 above.

[3]CTS editions: see Annex 2.

[4]Human work: *Gaudium et Spes* §§63-64 and 67 (pages 75-76 below); *Laborem Exercens* (page 129).

[5]Competition, etc: on these and other topics, see also the Index.

[6]Church's teaching on morals: see also Canon 747.2 of the *Code of Canon Law* (page 159).

[7]Employers and *owners:* e.g. sole and part-owners of businesses; partners, shareholders.

[8]Subsidiarity: see note [2] above.

MATER ET MAGISTRA

Mother and Teacher

1961

Encyclical Letter of Pope John XXIII

"Mother and Teacher of all nations – such is the Catholic Church in the mind of her Founder, Jesus Christ, to hold the world in an embrace of love..." These are the opening lines of this encyclical.

When in 1958 the cardinals in conclave, none of them young, elected to the papacy a man older than some of themselves, the man aged seventy-seven who took the name John XXIII, it was suggested that they saw him as a caretaker. If they did, Pope John XXIII must have surprised them, for he blended his shrewdness and long experience with the adventurousness and openness of youth.

Pope John XXIII had been in office only three months when he announced his plan to bring about a rare event – a General Council.[1] The Council began under his guidance in 1962 and opened doors to development and renewal throughout the Catholic Church.

Pope John's teaching had about it something of the freshness of the Christian gospel in which the Church's doctrine is always grounded. His language and style were simpler and friendlier than those used by some of his predecessors. These qualities can be tasted in Pope John's encyclicals. The two that include material concerning economic and social matters are examples: *Mater et Magistra* and *Pacem in Terris*.[2]

Mater et Magistra reaffirms the right to private ownership of property and the social function inherent in the right. Pope John XXIII, however, does not place this topic first in his encyclical, as Leo XIII did in *Rerum Novarum*. Among the changes in the world between 1891 and 1961 were two: the campaign of Marxists and others for transfer of ownership to the State lost some of its force and threat; and in Western countries millions of men and women emerged from the oppression and poverty of the nineteenth century and began to be seen as people of significance: as voters and trade union members for example; as consumers; and as owners of cars, boats, caravans, televisions, houses, shares and businesses. Millions began themselves to become private owners of property.

Responding to these changes, Pope John in *Mater et Magistra* gives special attention to the development and responsibility of the individual, alone and in association with others; and he places most of his paragraphs on these topics before his paragraphs on property. We see here – as in later documents[3] – an example of change of emphasis or priority which both maintains and develops the teaching of the Church.

Ten years after *Mater et Magistra* Pope John XXIII's successor referred to John's teaching thus: "He stressed how much the admittance to responsibility is a basic demand of human nature, an exercise of freedom and a path to human development. He showed how, in economic life and particularly in enterprise, this sharing in responsibilities should be ensured."[4]

Glancing for a moment backwards from Pope John after that look forwards, one may note in *Mater et Magistra* his affirmations of the teaching of his immediate predecessor Pius XII as well as of Pius XI and Leo XIII. Pius XII reigned from 1939. His broadcast of 1941 on the fiftieth anniversary of *Rerum Novarum* went into the noise of war. Other addresses of his had the same competition; then there was war's aftermath. And though Pius XII certainly contributed to social doctrine, the contribution was mainly oral. The capture of some of this in *Mater et Magistra* is a further service from Pope John XXIII.[4a]

The summary below of parts of Pope John's encyclical begins with *Individual and State* and *Social growth*. Under the second heading is the Pope's welcome for self-governing associations and movements, prominent in the third or central sphere of life referred to in the Introduction to the present work.[5] The name Social Growth is gratefully adopted from Winstone's translation,[6] in preference to another translation of the Latin *socialium rationum incrementa*, viz. "socialization", a word misleading as well as ugly, for its suggests ideological, political or State action of kinds not suggested by Pope John. According to Joseph Kirwan, writing in 1984 in his study-edition of *Laborem Exercens*, "socialization" in Italian and other versions of *Mater et Magistra* caused upset and confusion; and "John himself was careful never to speak of socialization in either Latin or Italian".[7] Sadly, the Second Vatican Council's *Gaudium et Spes* (whose drafters had *Mater et Magistra*, published but two or three years earlier, in the material before them) picked up the unlovely word, though perhaps with a grimace: "Socialization, as it is called,..."[8] May what was picked up be dropped, for good.

A further reason to drop socialization is that three popes later, in a recipe for fresh confusion, some translators of John Paul II again use "socialization", or "socializing", for a concept connected with social growth but distinct from it, viz. communal or shared ownership – *collatio in commune*. As before, according to Kirwan, the Pope himself refrains from speaking of socialization.[9]

From a section of *Mater et Magistra* chiefly concerned with agriculture comes paragraph 140, summarized below under the heading Pay. Pope John's family were small farmers. He examines agriculture as a sector of the economy sometimes unjustly treated, in comparison with other sectors. The principles he suggests may of course be applicable to other examples of unfairness, as regards certain classes of product or service.

Pope John had a feeling for both the divine and the down-to-earth. He remembers the person sometimes forgotten by teachers of social doctrine for the economy: he remembers the customer. See for example his references to the customer in two of the paragraphs summarized on page 55 below. See also his paragraphs under the preceding heading *Business: the common good*.

As employee or employer, as director, owner or investor, we take pay, profit and other returns, to sustain ourselves, our families and our businesses, and our lifestyle. These takings mean price to the customer. If the customer is rich the price may not matter. Many customers, however, are not rich; many in Britain, and on the Continent; many more overseas. Many, perhaps, will never be customers of Britain's at all (nor will their missing business give us employment) unless we can find a way to moderate our prices.

The reader may like to link Pope John's teaching with the social doctrine's call to us to live its principles not only in special activities such as public campaigns, and support for charities, but in our economic everyday; with the call to contribute competence in our ordinary work; with the invitation of John Paul II to consider the influence we have as "indirect employers in the socio-economic system" (see pages 132-133, 140-141 below); and with the calls from the Second Vatican Council, Paul VI and John Paul II for a preference for the poor.

A less costly lifestyle, for some of us; readiness to work for lesser increases in profit, pay and other returns; whence lesser increases in the sums our businesses have to cover, and fewer increases in prices to customers; and better competence from us in British business, so that we learn how to meet customers' needs less expensively – could action such as this be some part of an answer to the calls?

After considering responsibility, property and the other matters, *Mater et Magistra* commends the Church's social doctrine and offers advice for putting it into practice. In the two sections with which our summary ends, Pope John like Leo and Pius before him is not ashamed to recall his readers, living amid ever-modern excitements and problems, to principles as old as Christianity itself; principles which in one form or another are probably as old as all wisdom.

MATER ET MAGISTRA

Individual and State

§§51-58 (74, 117). "In the economic order first place must be given to the personal initiative of private citizens working either as individuals or in association with each other... for the furtherance of common interests."

The State, guided by the principle of subsidiary function,[10] and responsible for the common good, must also have a hand in the economy. "But however extensive and far-reaching the influence of the State may be, it must never be exerted to the extent of depriving the individual citizen of his freedom of action. It must rather augment his freedom by effectively guaranteeing the protection of his essential personal rights. Among these is a person's right and duty to be primarily responsible for his own upkeep and that of his family. Hence every economic system must permit and facilitate the free development of productive activity."

Where personal initiative is lacking, political tyranny ensues, and economic stagnation in production, and in services of the material and spiritual order – those dependent on individual creative talent.

Where on the other hand the good offices of the State are deficient, disorder ensues; in particular, exploitation of the weak by the strong.

Social growth[11]

§§59-67. To attain objectives beyond the means of single individuals, we join others in associations, movements and institutions for economic, social and other ends. In this way we make it possible for the individual to exercise personal rights, "especially those we call economic and social, such as the right to the means of obtaining a livelihood, preserving good health, receiving further education and a more thorough professional training; the right to housing, work, leisure and recreation..."

We should manage this social growth so as to minimize constraints upon individual freedom and responsibility. "To this end... public authority must take account of all those social conditions which favour the full development of human personality. Moreover, We consider it altogether vital that intermediary bodies[12] and corporate enterprises – which are, so to say, the main vehicle of this social growth – be really autonomous, and work loyally in pursuit both of their own interests and of the common good... and... treat their individual members as human persons and encourage them to take an active part in the ordering of their lives." Governments should strike a balance "between the autonomous and active collaboration of individuals and groups, and the timely coordination and encouragement of private enterprise by the State."

Social action in accord with these principles is likely to help individuals develop their personal talents.

Responsibility, opportunity, self-development

§§55, 62, 83, 84, 90-92, 96, 112, 145, 151, 158, 240-241, 253. Our role in the economy carries personal responsibility: acceptance and fulfilment of our own responsibility; helping others to accept and fulfil theirs; and giving others a share in responsibility.

§§150-184. There are opportunities for individuals, alone and in association (as well as for States) in helping build or rebuild local or national economies which are underdeveloped or in need, at home or abroad.

§§254-256, 259.   Commitment to our daily responsibilities can readily harmonize with our human and spiritual development. "It is a gross error to suppose that a man cannot perfect himself except by putting aside earthly activity..." That we should develop and perfect ourself through our daily work is completely in keeping with God's plan. Our work can be a continuation of God's own.

Pay

§§70-72.   Pay must be in accordance with justice. It must allow a truly human life, and fulfilment of family obligations. Other factors: the worker's contribution to the good of the community and to production, profits and the economy; the financial state of the business; the good of the country (especially employment) and of the family of nations; the quantity and quality of available resources.

§140.   Even if produce is of a kind required in order to satisfy primary needs, so that the price should be within the means of all consumers – e.g. farm produce – we must not use this as an argument for keeping a section of the population – e.g. farm workers – in a permanent state of economic and social inferiority.

Economy – society – individual

§§73-74.   Social progress must accompany economic, so that all classes participate in increased productivity.

The national economy has no other purpose than to secure the conditions in which the individual life of the citizen may fully develop. The economic prosperity of a nation is not so much its total wealth as equitable distribution, for the personal development of the members of society.

Profit and growth

§§75-77.   As Pius XI taught,[13] it is unjust for capital or labour to claim all the profits. Thus companies putting profit back into growth should recognize their employees' share in it. We can achieve justice here in many ways, especially by sharing in the ownership of the businesses in which we work.

Business: the common good

§§78-81.   We must not consider only the claims of pay and of profit, within business. We must also consider the common good, at home and abroad.[14]

The demands of the common good include employment, for the greatest number; balance between pay and prices; the need to make goods and services accessible[15] to the greatest number; balance between economic expansion and social services; adjustment to the progress of science and technology; the development of less advanced economies; and "the need to make the prosperity of a more human way of life available not only to the present generation but to coming generations as well".

We must also consider the common good when assessing interest, dividends, and rewards to directors.

Humanness, participation and service

§§82-103, 142-149, (62-65).   "...Every person has, of their
very nature, a need to express themself in their work and thereby
to perfect their own being. Consequently, if the structure and
organization of an economic system is such as to compromise
human dignity, to lessen sense of responsibility or rob of
opportunity for exercising personal initiative, then such a system
is altogether unjust – no matter how much wealth it produces,
or how justly and equitably such wealth is distributed."

Small businesses, farms and other family businesses, and
cooperatives, are examples offering scope for fostering dignity, responsibility and initiative. In larger concerns, job-
contracts can develop towards partnership. We should have
some kind of real participation and share in the business in
which we work, be the business private or public. We should
have a say in, and make a contribution to, the running and
development of the enterprise. In business we must maintain
efficient directive unity; but we must not treat employees as
cogs in machinery, denying them opportunity to express their
wishes and to bring their experience to bear.

All of us – management and employees – should work not
so much for what we can get out of the business as for what we
can give in service to colleagues and to customers.[16]

Change – education and training – influence

§§87-88, 94-95.   We must adjust equipment and method to
changes in science and technology and to changes in the
demands and preferences of the customer. We should make
more time for technical and professional training and for
cultural, moral and religious education.

§§97-99, 143-146.   Employees and their representatives, no
less than management, should exert influence with the
authorities and institutions whose decisions affect the
economy.

Property

§§109-121.   The right to private ownership of property, including the means of production, has permanent validity. It is a guarantee of freedom of the individual; a means of asserting personality and exercising responsibility. We should extend it to all classes of citizen, to cover for example consumer durables, houses, land, tools and equipment, and shares.

Inherent in the right is its social function: we hold what we own for the benefit of others, as well as for self. Helpful efforts by individuals and private groups promote spiritual values better than public authority can.

Public authority, private enterprise

§§150-152.   Public authority should promote employment and enterprise. Whilst acting to help underdeveloped areas in the economy, Authority should treat the citizens of these areas as responsible human beings who play the major role in achieving their own economic, social and cultural advancement.

"Private enterprise too must contribute to economic and social balance... Indeed, in accordance with the principle of subsidiary function,[17] public authority must encourage and assist private enterprise, entrusting to it, wherever possible, the continuation of economic development."

Responsibility – material and spiritual

§§157-158, 163-165, 175-177.   We who are more blessed with this world's goods must educate our conscience to the responsibility of each and every one for the citizens of countries that are poverty-stricken. All those who help train these people in economic and social development or who help provide capital for economic enterprise in these countries are doing a magnificent work.

At the same time we must remember that scientific and technical progress, economic development and the betterment of living conditions, though certainly valuable in civilization, are essentially instrumental: they are not supreme values in themselves. "It pains Us, therefore, to observe the complete indifference to the true hierarchy of values shown by so many people in the economically developed countries. Spiritual values are ignored, forgotten or denied, while the progress of science, technology and economics is pursued for its own sake, as though material well-being were the be-all and end-all of life. This attitude is contagious, especially when it infects the work that is being done for the underdeveloped countries, which have often preserved in their ancient traditions an acute and vital awareness of the more important human values.

"To attempt to undermine this national integrity is certainly immoral. It must be respected and as far as possible clarified and developed, so that it may remain what it is: a foundation of true civilization."

Material progress: ideologies

§§212-217. All the scientific, technical and economic progress we can make will not bring justice and peace until we return to a sense of our dignity[18] as daughters and sons of God. Ideologies are proving less and less attractive: they do not take account of the whole of a human being, nor even of the most important part.

The social doctrine

§§218-221. "Catholic social teaching rests on one basic principle: individual human beings are the foundation, the cause and the purpose of every social institution." We are by nature social beings. By God's design we are also raised to an order of reality which is above nature.

"On this principle, which guarantees the dignity of the individual, the Church constructs the whole of her social teaching." The doctrine takes into account human nature, the varying conditions in which human life is lived, and the characteristics of society.

§§222-226. "This Catholic social doctrine is an integral part of the Christian conception of life... Its light is Truth, Justice its objective, Love[19] its driving force."

§§223-227. "It is Our urgent desire that this social doctrine be studied more and more." Lay Christians, individually and working with others, should join priests and teachers in studying it and in putting it into practice.[19a]

Christian education and training

§§228-232. Christian education must foster awareness of the duty to carry on economic and social activities in a Christian manner. Moving from theory to practice is especially hard in face of selfishness, materialism, and the difficulty sometimes in determining just what the demands of justice are in a given instance.

We should learn through practical training as well as theoretical instruction, and through our own action. "One learns Christian behaviour in social and economic matters by Christian action in those fields."

Putting into practice

§236. There are three stages we should normally follow in putting social principles into practice. First, review the facts of the situation; second, form a judgement in the light of the principles; third, decide what in the circumstances can and should be done to implement them. Look, judge, act.

§§241-7, (175-77). Lay Christians should not only be well qualified in their daily occupation: they should also bring their working lives into conformity with the Church's teaching, and not lose sight of true values. "Scientific and technical progress, and the resultant material well-being, are good things and mark an important phase in human civilization; but they must be valued according to their nature." They are only instruments, to be used in ways that serve our true humanness and destiny.

Christian life

§§234-5. The Christian conception of life demands a spirit of moderation and sacrifice. Pleasure and satisfaction, alone, have evil effects.

§§248-53. Bodily as well as spiritual refreshment, and family life, recommend the keeping of Sunday.[20]

NOTES
[Page numbers refer to pages in this book]

[1]General Council: see Introduction to *Gaudium et Spes* (page 66). For a second surprise sprung by Pope John XXIII, see page 155.

[2]See page 61.

[3]See for example the text and context of the paragraphs on property in *Gaudium et Spes* §§69-71 (page 78), in *Laborem Exercens* §§63-69 (page 139), and in *Sollicitudo Rei Socialis* §42 (page 170).

[4]Paul VI, *Octogesima Adveniens* §47 (page 110). Pope Paul VI also refers to *Gaudium et Spes* §§68 and 75 (pages 77, 79).

[4a]Pius XII: see e.g. §§41-45, 74, 84, 92, 111, 114, 181, 243 in *Mater et Magistra* (not all summarized in the present work). Pius XII gets attention in the excellent *L'Economie, L'Homme, La Societé* by Jean-Yves Calvez (see Annex 2).

[5]Third or central sphere: see page 18.

[6]H.E. Winstone's translation is published by the Catholic Truth Society: see Annex 2. For some reason Fr. Winstone (or an editor?) inserted Socialization as a heading to Pope John XXIII's paragraphs 59-67 – a heading not contained in the orginal, according to a note printed in the CTS revised edition of 1963. Happily however, in translating the paragraphs themselves, Winstone shuns socialization and uses social growth (§65) and similar phrases.

[7]Kirwan, p. 69: see Annex 2, *Laborem Exercens*.

[8]*Gaudium et Spes* §25.

[9]Kirwan, p. 68; *Laborem Exercens* §§65-69 (page 139).

[10]Subsidiary function: see pages 20-21 and 45.

[11]Social Growth: see pages 18, 49-50.

[12]"Intermediary Bodies": groups working between the lone individual and the State, such as associations for education, for training, and for commercial and professional standards; business and other enterprises; trade unions; clubs, institutions, movements, organizations, societies, trusts. See Introduction (page 18).

[13]Pius XI: see page 44.

[14]Common Good: for example the claims of on the one hand those of us in business (labour, management and capital together) and on the other hand the community, the economy, customers rich and poor at home and abroad, and the whole human family.

[15]Accessible – e.g. to customers, at reasonable prices.

[16]Service: see also *Gaudium et Spes* §64 (page 75). *Redemptor Hominis* §21 (pages 123-124).

[17]Subsidiary function: see pages 20-21, 45.

[18]Dignity: prime meaning, viz. true worth, excellence.

[19]Love its driving force: see pages 24-32.

[19a]Study: see *Apostolicam Actuositatem* §§31, 32 and note, pages 86, 87.

[20]Sunday: reconfirmed yet again by John Paul II in 1988: "Keeping to this rhythm at once human and divine – six days' work, one of rest – is as though we continue the work of the Creator" (Address to industrial workers in Civita Castellana, *L'Osservatore Roman*, 23 May 1988).

PACEM IN TERRIS

Peace Throughout the World

1963

Encyclical Letter of Pope John XXIII

"An Encyclical Letter on building peace throughout the world on truth, justice, love and freedom": words from the title Pope John gave to *Pacem in Terris*, his last encyclical. He signed it in April 1963, six months after doctors had warned him he had not too much longer to live. Then, as reported of him: "My bags are packed. I'm ready to go." He died in June.

The headings chosen by editors for the five parts of *Pacem in Terris* indicate its scope –

    I   Relationships between individuals
    II   Citizen and State
    III   Relations between States
    IV   The world community
    V   Conclusions

The pages that follow here summarize the encyclical's teaching on the role of the individual.

Pope John's words about education – the closing topic summarized below – may have particular pertinence for Britain. Lecturing and writing apart, the present author has not worked in education; nor has he experienced parenthood. His impression as an interested citizen, however, is that many of our young people, after long years at home with their parents and costly years in our schools and colleges, step into the world with little or no education in Christian social doctrine, and with little or none in the Christian mode of learning and life, essential to understanding; the mode used by Christ and given its potential for fruitfulness by the Holy Spirit.[1] From the blank looks on the faces of some Catholics, if conversation ever turns to Christian social doctrine or modes of learning,

the author wonders if the voids yawn in some families and
schools supposedly Catholic, as well as in others.

The Church in General Council has recognized that education for responsibility begins in the family, and has confirmed
the duty of parents to "promote integrated, personal *and social*
education of their children".[2] The Church has reminded us that
training for Christ's work should continue through adolescence, school, youth, and the whole of life, and that this training should also include self-education, especially as self-
awareness expands in adulthood.[3] The Church calls for study
of her social teaching in particular.[4]

The Church has also affirmed her own obligation "to provide for her children an education by virtue of which *their
whole lives* may be inspired by the spirit of Christ"[5] – an
obligation for everyone who works with the Church in education, and not just for bishops, priests, and teachers who are in
religious orders.

The calls of popes and of British bishops for study of the
social doctrine have already been noted.[6]

Parents, teachers, and the rest of us: have we heeded?

PACEM IN TERRIS

§§1-10.   We will have peace only if we observe the order
designed by God to guide relationships between individuals,
between citizen and authority, and between states – an order
designed by him to be discoverable in our heart, mind, and
conscience. By the same design, every one of us is endowed
with intelligence and free will, and has rights and duties which
flow directly from our human nature and are universal, inviolable and inalienable.

Rights[7]

§§11-27.   The rights of every person include the rights
   – to the means for decent living
   – to freedom to seek truth, and to follow a vocation

- to good education, and training, and to a share in the benefits of culture[8]
- to opportunity to work and to exercise initiative at work; and to reasonable working conditions.

They include also the rights
- to go responsibly into business
- to be paid what is just and sufficient for earner and family
- to own property, including productive property
- to form and join associations, and through them to exercise initiative and responsibility
- to have freedom of movement and residence
- to participate in public affairs.

§19.   Women must be accorded conditions of work consistent with their needs and responsibilities as wives and mothers.

§24.   Associations intermediate between individual and State, for the pursuit of aims we cannot achieve as loners, are essential for personal freedom, dignity, and responsibility.

Rights and duties

§44.   Awareness of rights leads to recognition of duties.

§§28-29, 30-33, 44.   Rights bring duties of two kinds: the duties of each person that are the other side of her or his own rights; and the duties each has to respect and respond to the rights of others.

§§29, 22.   Examples of the first kind are the duties to lead a decent life, and to seek truth. The social obligations of ownership are a further example.

§§30-33.   An example of the second kind is the duty to do all we can – alone, and joining with others – to see that the means of livelihood are available to everyone.

Requirements

§§34-38, 48, 60.   Recognition of rights, observance of duties, and collaboration with others should be primarily matters of personal decision, each of us acting on our own initiative, conviction, and sense of responsibility. There is nothing human about a society that is welded together by force. Society must be based on truth, and will be, if we each acknowledge our rights and duties.

Human society demands justice, love, freedom, and responsibility, and is thus primarily a spiritual reality having its origin in God, the deepest source from which human society can draw genuine vitality.

§§48-65.   An important requirement upon the State is to ensure fair and favourable conditions for enjoyment of rights and fulfilment of duties by all its citizens in freedom, and for contribution to the common good, material and spiritual, by individuals and groups.

Christians: competence, integration

§§146-164.   Taking care to acquire and contribute competence, Christians in their work should try to help every enterprise and institution – economic, social or other – to foster and not obstruct human self-betterment. Christians have a special obligation to set an example in the world.

In our daily lives we must be conscious of personal rights and duties. We must integrate spiritual values with those of science, technology and the professions.

Education

§153.   The thinness of secondary education in Christian religion and morality, compared with the attention we give to other subjects, is a cause of breach between faith and practice. We should remedy this. Our education should be both balanced and sustained, so that growth in religious knowledge and moral integrity keeps pace with scientific knowledge and technical skill.

NOTES
[Page numbers refer to pages in this book]

[1]See Index: Holy Spirit.

[2]Second Vatican Council, 1965: *Gravissimum Educationis* (not summarized in this book) §3.

[3]*Apostolicam Actuositatem* §§30-32 (page 86).

[4]*Apostolicam Actuositatem* §31(b). Again in 1988: see pages 181-182.

[5]*Gravissimum Educationis* §3.

[6]See pages 14, 58. See also e.g. pages 107, 181-182.

[7]Rights: in its paragraphs 11-28 the CTS Winstone translation of *Pacem in Terris* (see Annex 2) uses mostly the simple word "right"; four times "natural right"; once "inherent right". Current general usage might name all the rights treated in these paragraphs as *human rights*, since as Pope John XXIII presents them they flow directly from our human nature – and not for example from decision or law of the State. Paragraph 68 of *Gaudium et Spes* (to take a different and particular context – see page 77) uses "fundamental right". Study of right and duty in the social doctrine is however beyond the scope of this book, which looks rather at the doctrine's emphasis on opportunity and responsibility.

[8]See Note [3] to *Gaudium et Spes* (page 79).

GAUDIUM ET SPES

The Church in the Modern World

1965

Pastoral Constitution of the Second Vatican Council

In contrast to papal letters, *Gaudium et Spes* is a document of a General Council of the Catholic Church, in this instance the Second Vatican Council. A General Council is a working conference of the bishops and others with similar responsibilities in the churches of the Roman communion, from all parts of the world. It works with the authority and guidance of the Pope, and is assisted by experts in theology and in other sciences and disciplines.

General Councils are rare. The Council previous to Vatican II was held nearly a century before, the first to be held in the Vatican. The Council previous to Vatican I was three centuries earlier still, at Trent.

Vatican II began in October 1962 under Pope John XXIII. He died in 1963. The Council continued under Paul VI and ended in December 1965. On its twentieth anniversary in 1985 Vatican II was celebrated and its implementation was reviewed at an Extraordinary Synod of Bishops, attended by John Paul II.

Pope John XXIII summoned Vatican II to consider and present the Church's authentic teaching through the methods and forms of twentieth-century thought. He reminded the bishops of the true, high worth of our human nature and purpose, and invited them to explain the Church's understanding, as a help to fully human living for everyone, believer and unbeliever, in this modern world of progress, promise and danger.[1]

Among the sixteen constitutions, decrees and other documents that register the work of Vatican II, the Constitution *Gaudium et Spes* responds with especial readiness to Pope John XXIII's invitation. In the years that have passed since Vatican II, *Gaudium et Spes* is one of the documents to which successor-popes refer frequently. Pope Paul VI in *Populorum Progressio* and Pope John Paul II in *Sollicitudo Rei Socialis* furnish examples.[2] John Paul II has also many times referred to *Gaudium et Spes* in his homilies at Mass, and in his audiences and addresses given to the public and to specialists.

This conciliar document has the official title *De Ecclesia in mundo huius temporis*, usually translated as *The Church in the Modern World*. Like the document's papal cousins, however, it is more often known by the opening words of its Latin: *Gaudium et Spes* – Joy and Hope. In English the opening sentences read:

"The joy and hope, the grief and anguish of the men and women of our time, especially of those who are poor or afflicted in any way, are the joy and hope, the grief and anguish of the followers of Christ as well. Nothing that is genuinely human fails to find an echo in their hearts."

In English translation *Gaudium et Spes* runs to some ninety-five pages, arranged as Preface and Introduction, Part One, Part Two, and Conclusion. In the light of Christian belief and understanding, Part One examines our human dignity, nature, role, responsibilities and needs, as individuals and as members of the community; the partnership with himself which God offers us; the links between service and self-development; our opportunities when we live in accord with God's design and love. Part One also reaffirms yet again God's censure upon the notion that Christians should be concerned only for the next world.

Part Two examines five matters: marriage and family; culture[3]; economic and social life; politics; peace and the international community.

Part One contains little that is explicitly and exclusively economic, but much that is pertinent to the economic no less than to every other department of our lives. Part One is of first importance in the Church's social doctrine. Knowledge of Part One is also essential to good understanding of the treatment given by Part Two to its particular matters.

The text after this introduction condenses the paragraphs of the Constitution of importance to the role of the individual alone and with others in the economy. This means that nearly all paragraphs treated are from Part One and from only the

third topic of Part Two – Economic and Social Life. A short
summary might be this:

1. The earth and all it contains – nature's resources, and our
products – exist to serve the fulfilment of every human being,
as an individual and as a member of the community.
2. Justice, love, and responsibility, individual and social, are
the chief means at our disposal for ensuring that these good
things do serve this fulfilment.
3. The design is God's. Despite our failings, Jesus Christ and
the Holy Spirit offer to every person of good will, believer and
unbeliever, a share of God's own strength to live and work in
partnership with this design.

The first of these teachings is named by phrases such as the
Universal Destination (or Purpose) of Earthly Goods. Paragraph 69 of *Gaudium et Spes* contains one of the best known
statements of it. The doctrine is applied in further contexts in
*Populorum Progressio, Laborem Exercens, Sollicitudo Rei
Socialis,* and *Christifideles Laici.*[4]
There is a paragraph in Part Two, in the chapter on economic and social life, which is pertinent both ˙o a poisonous
disorder of our time – unemployment – and to the matter of
individual responsibility. Paragraph 67, as summarized below, declares: "We have duty and right to work. It is also our
duty in society, according to circumstances, to ensure opportunity to work, for our fellow citizens." The Council sees a
duty of society; not of government alone. Words to similar
effect can be found in other paragraphs also: 65, 68, 70, 71
and 75 for example, and at the end of 69 (summarized below
with 75).
Pope John XXIII likewise saw social growth, rather than
government action alone, as important for the exercise of
personal rights, "especially those we call economic and social, such as the right to the means of obtaining a livelihood...
and a more thorough professional training; the right to housing and work..."[5]
Pope John Paul II makes the point again in *Laborem Exercens,*[6] in *Christifideles Laici,*[7] and again in 1988: "Work is a
right. When *society* and authorities fail to do what they can to

overcome unemployment, a right is denied."[8] "The right and duty of all persons to have or obtain work is clear. Equally clear is the duty of *social groups and society as a whole* to do all in their power to ensure that no one is without work."[9]

So too the Instruction on *Christian Freedom and Liberation*: "The fact that unemployment keeps large sectors of the population and notably the young in a situation of marginalization is intolerable. The creation of jobs is a primary social task for individuals and private enterprise, as well as the State".[10]

GAUDIUM ET SPES
Part One

The dignity[11] of the human person

§§12, (25, 64, 69).   Men and women have been created in the image of God, able to know and love our maker, and appointed by him masters of all lesser creatures and of all creation's resources. We have also been made social beings: we cannot live or develop our talents except in relationships with others.

§§13, (10, 25).   We abuse our freedom, and are drawn towards pride, selfishness and wrongdoing: individual and social life is a struggle between good and evil. But Jesus Christ came to strengthen and to inwardly renew us.

§§14, 15.   The interior insights and resources within every human being can bring understanding of more than our bodies, more than material and visible things, more than technology and the discoveries of science. Every one of us can also seek, find and love greater realities, such as goodness and truth.

People poor in material goods can be richer in wisdom than people advanced in science and technology.[12]

Conscience, freedom and faith

§§16, 17, 21.5.   If we take trouble to discover and try to live what is true and good, we will find in our conscience[13] the law fulfilled in love of God and neighbour, telling us inwardly at the right moment: do this, shun that. Then, given freedom, we can choose what is good in the way appropriate to our human dignity, that is, consciously and freely, neither by blind impulse nor from external constraint.

"Faith should show its fruitfulness by penetrating the whole life of believers, their worldly activity included; urging them to be loving and just, especially towards those in need."

Renewal

§§22, (10, 13, 37, 38).   Our dignity and mission are best seen in Jesus Christ. Jesus, fully human as well as divine, shows that self-giving love opens a way for us to receive the Holy Spirit, who can empower us too to fulfil the new law of love[14] and can inwardly renew our whole self, despite evil, weakness, wrongdoing, suffering, and death.

All this is true not only for Christians but also for all people of goodwill in whose hearts grace is active. Christ died for all of us, and the Holy Spirit offers to all the possibility of being made partners in God's work of restoration.

Individual and society

§§24, 25 (35).   The first and greatest commandment – of paramount importance in a world of growing interdependence – is to love God and neighbour. We cannot fully find our true self except in self-giving. Life in society is essential to us; not accessory. Advancement of personality and of society go hand in hand. In mutual service, our talents grow.

Economic, political and social tensions are a cause of troubles: deeper causes are selfishness, pride, and sin.

The common good

§§26, (63, 86b). As interdependence grows, so does the point of "the common good", which is "the sum total of social conditions which allow people, as groups or as individuals, to reach fulfilment more fully and more easily".[15] Every group must take into account the needs and aspirations of every other group, and of the whole human family.

At the same time, because of the dignity of the human person, the individual has rights and duties that are universal and inviolable. Every human being should have ready access to everything necessary for living a truly human life, including food, clothes, housing, education, work, respect, and the right to act according to a correct conscience.[16]

"The social order and its development must yield to the good of the person, since the order of things must be subordinate to the order of persons and not the other way round..." We must constantly improve the social order, in truth, justice, and love. We should renew our attitudes; change our mentality.

§§27, (66). We must have respect for one another, and for our neighbours' needs for a decent quality of life. We must make ourself the neighbour of every person in need whom we can help. Whatever offends human dignity, such as subhuman living conditions, or treatment of employees as mere tools for profit instead of free, responsible men and women: these and the like poison civilization.

Discrimination, disparity

§§29, (66). All human beings have the same divine calling and destiny: a basic equality that must be given ever greater recognition. Discrimination in basic personal rights on grounds of sex, race, colour, class, language or religion is contrary to God's design: we must root it out. We must strive for fairer and more humane conditions. Excessive economic and social disparity between individuals and peoples militates against social justice, human dignity, and peace.

Individualistic morality

§30. No one today should be content to lounge in a merely individualistic morality. The best way to fulfil our obligations of justice and love is to contribute to the common good, and to promote and help public and private organizations working for better conditions of life.

Dishonest avoidance of just taxes; dangerous flouting of speed limits: faults like these are out of tune with the morality needed today. We should all count social obligations important among present-day duties.

Responsibility, solidarity

§§31, 32. Extremes of lifestyle, high or wretched, can dull our sense of responsibility and blunt the awareness of our human dignity and calling to service in the community. God has designed us for solidarity.

In developing education for responsibility we must above all help young people from all social backgrounds to become the kind of men and women needed by our times: men and women not only of culture but of great personality as well.

Partnership with God

§§34, (43, 57, 67). Human achievement through the centuries to develop the world and improve human living is in tune with God's design.[17] In our daily work too, when we provide for ourselves and our families and serve the community, we can look upon our work as a continuation of the work of the Creator, a service to our fellows, and our personal contribution to the fulfilment in history of the divine plan. As our powers grow, so do our responsibilities, as individuals and as communities.

Development and self-development

§§35, (57). In our work and service we not only transform the world: we fulfil ourselves. We learn, we develop our faculties, we emerge and go beyond ourselves. This kind of growth is the best wealth. It is what we are that counts, rather than what we have.[18]
Technical advance is of less value than progress towards greater justice, wider fellowship, and a more humane social environment. Technical advance may supply material for human progress but is powerless to achieve it.

Love[19]

§§37, 38, 39 (22). The fundamental law of human perfection and hence of the transformation of the world is the new commandment of love. The way of love is open to everyone.
This love is not something reserved for important matters, but must be exercised above all in the ordinary circumstances of daily life.
Despite the infections of evil and sin in the world, despite the crosses we have to carry, Christ with the authority of his resurrection is at work in our hearts by the power of his Spirit. Not only does he arouse desire for the world to come but he stimulates, purifies and strengthens our generous and unselfish aspirations to make our present life more human and to bring the earth's resources into the service of this more human life.
Nourishment and refreshment for this work, and a foretaste of the celebration there will be when it is completed, are offered in the Mass. On this earth the body of a new human family is growing, foreshadowing the age to come.

Christian faith: earthly responsibility

§§43, (30, 31, 34, 57, 65, 67, 68, 69, 71, 72, 21.5). Christian faith sharpens the duty to fulfil earthly responsibilities. We have personal responsibility in the economy and in society, as well as in our private lives.

"It is a mistake to think that because we have here 'no lasting city, but seek the city which is to come',[20] we are entitled to shirk earthly responsibilities: by our faith we are bound all the more to fulfil these responsibilities according to the vocation of each person. It is no less mistaken to think that we may immerse ourselves in earthly activities as if these were foreign to religion, and religion nothing more than acts of worship and a few moral obligations. One of the worst errors of our time is the breach between the faith many profess and the practice of their daily lives" – a breach Christ threatens with severe punishment.[21] "The Christian who shirks his earthly duties neglects his duties to his neighbour, neglects God, and endangers his eternal salvation."

Christians should follow the example of Christ, who worked as a craftsman.[22] We should integrate our human effort – at work, in the family and outside, in culture[23] and in science and technology – with religious values.

We should not be satisfied with meeting minimum legal requirements: we should strive to become truly competent in our activities. Christians should gladly cooperate with others working towards the same objectives, should show initiative and shoulder responsibilities.

GAUDIUM ET SPES
Part Two

Education for responsibility

§§48, 52. Education begins in the family. Parents have a prime responsibility for the education of their children. Parents' example also, and family prayer, are important in helping the young find the way to maturity and fulfilment.

Education should be such as to help children to live responsibly when they grow up and, if they marry, to found their own family in favourable circumstances moral, social and economic.[24]

Values of modern culture

§57.   Among the positive values of modern culture are fidelity to truth in scientific investigation, team work in technology, sense of international solidarity, awareness of the expert's responsibility to help and defend his fellow men, and an eagerness to improve standards of living, especially of those deprived of responsibility or suffering cultural destitution.

Our role in the economy

§63.   In the economic and social sphere of our life, no less than any other, we must respect and foster the dignity of the human person as well as the welfare of society. Human beings are the source, focus and object of all economic and social life.

Our growing mastery over nature, and better productivity, distribution and services make a modern economy an instrument capable of meeting the growing needs of the human family; yet all is not well. Many of us allow ourselves to be dominated by economics, permeated with a kind of economic mentality. Economic progress too often increases inequalities when it could reduce them; it even worsens the position of the poor. Luxury and misery exist side by side. The growing contrast between the economically advanced countries and others could endanger world peace.

All this can and should be rectified by the greater technical and economic resources available in the world today; but we need to reform our economic and social life. We need to change our mentality and attitude.

§64.   Economic and technical progress, the spirit of enterprise, creativity, improvement, production: we must indeed foster all these. Their purpose, however, is not just production increase, profit or prestige, but the service of human beings, "of man in his totality", taking into account our needs material, intellectual, moral, spiritual and religious, worldwide. So that God's design for us may be fulfilled, we must manage our economic activities within morality.

§65.   We should not leave development to the judgement of a few individuals or groups possessing too much economic power, nor of the political community alone. "As many people as possible... should participate actively in decision-making." We should coordinate the voluntary initiatives of individuals and free groups, with public enterprises.

"Nor should development be left to the almost mechanical evolution of economic activity nor to the decision of public authority." Doctrines are wrong which obstruct reform on pretext of a false notion of freedom; and so are those which subordinate the basic rights of individuals and groups to the collective organization of production.[25]

All citizens have the right and duty to contribute, according to their ability, to the progress of their community. Authority must recognize this. In regions of retarded economic progress, especially, we endanger the common good if we hoard our resources or deprive the community of material and spiritual help.

§66.   For justice, we must try to put an end to huge and growing economic inequalities, and to individual and social discrimination. We must offer training for change, especially to the disadvantaged.

Work,[26] *pay and production*

§§67 (34, 43).   Human work, in the production and exchange of goods and in the provision of services, surpasses all other elements of economic life. Through work we can serve ourselves, our families and our fellows, put love into practice, and partner God in bringing his creative work to perfection.

We have duty and right to work. It is also our duty in

society,[27] according to circumstances, to ensure opportunity to work, for our fellow-citizens. With consideration to each person's job and productivity, to economic factors and the common good, pay must give adequate scope for personal and family life on the material, social, cultural and spiritual levels.

"It frequently happens, even today, that workers are almost enslaved by the work they do. So-called laws of economics are no excuse for this kind of thing. We must accommodate the entire process of productive work to human needs and lives, with special attention to domestic life and to mothers of families, taking sex and age always into account."

There should be scope to develop talent and personality in work. Giving time, energy and responsibility in our work, we should also have and allow to others sufficient rest, and leisure for family, for culture, and for social and religious life.

Participation: trade unions

§§68, (65). Taking into account the differing roles of all involved, and safeguarding singleness of management, we should encourage everybody who works in a business to share in the running of it. Directly or through representatives, those who work in business should also have a say in the economic and social decisions made by institutions at higher levels.

"Among the fundamental rights of the individual must be numbered the right of workers to form associations which truly represent them and are able to cooperate in organizing economic life properly, and the right to play a part in the activities of such associations without risk of reprisal. Thanks to such participation, along with economic and social education, awareness will grow among all people of their role and responsibility, and... they will feel they have an active part to play in the task of economic and social development and in the achievement of the common good."

In the event of dispute, we should strive first to settle by peaceful discussion. The strike remains a necessary last resort for defence of rights and satisfaction of rightful aspirations.[28]

Property, justice and love

§§69 (21.5, 86b, 88).   God destined the earth and all it contains for all human beings and peoples, to be shared fairly, in
justice and love, especially with those in need. "We must never
lose sight of this universal destination of earthly goods." Every
human being has the right to sufficient of the earth's goods for
self and family.

In the way we use it, we should regard what we own as
common to others also, for it can benefit others as well as
ourself. We have a duty to help the poor, and not merely from
what we do not need ourself.

"Feed those dying of hunger. If you do not feed them, you
are killing them": may individuals and governments remember this. We should, indeed, share and employ our assets to
help others.[29] Above all, we should help others to help and
develop themselves. We should make the necessary mental
and material adjustments.

§70.   When investing and planning, individuals[30] and associations as well as public authority must keep in mind employment present and future, other longer-term objectives, and
the needs of the poorer countries, as well as present-day
consumption.

§71.   Private property contributes to the expression of personality, and to individual and family freedom, independence
and security. Ownership by individuals and communities
should be fostered.

Private ownership also stimulates responsibility, and brings
opportunities for social and economic service. It has a social
dimension: paragraph 69 above.[31]

Christian example

§72.   Christians working for economic and social progress
should set an example of skill and experience, of a proper
sense of values, and of lives individual and social inspired by
the beatitudes, and in particular by the spirit of poverty.[32]

Individuals and the State

§§75, 69 (end). We should not give too much power to public authority, nor make excessive demands for benefits and subsidies, diminishing our own role. Family and social services should be further developed – especially services providing education and culture;[33] but they give no right to irresponsibility or refusal to do a fair share.

Government must protect and foster the rights, duties and constructive activities of individuals and families; of family, cultural and social groups; and of intermediary bodies[34] and institutions.

Conclusion

§93. Joining forces with all who love and practise justice, Christians can want nothing more ardently than to love and serve the men and women of our time, in word and deed: a task for which we must answer to God, who will judge every person. Not everyone who says, "Lord, Lord", will enter the kingdom of heaven, but those who do the will of the Father, and get down to the work.

NOTES
[Page numbers refer to pages in this book]

[1] See Pope John XXIII's *Humanae Salutis* of December 1961 convoking Vatican II and his address to the Council on its first day. English translations of both are printed in *The Documents of Vatican II* edited by Walter Abbot (see Annex 2, pages 193, 195).

[2] *Populorum Progressio* §§22, 48, 71 (pages 91, 93); *Sollicitudo Rei Socialis* §§26, 28, 33, 36, 42, 47 (pages 166-172).

[3] §§53-62 of *Gaudium et Spes* explain the wide meaning the Church sees in "culture", embracing everything that develops and refines our gifts of mind and body. They also explain the importance of this culture for every human being – not just for the artistically or intellectually superior.

[4]Universal Purpose of Goods: see pages 68, 78, 91, 139, 170, 180.

[5]Social Growth: see pages 49-50, 52.

[6]§§82-83 (page 141).

[7]§43, (page 180-181).

[8]Address at Civita Castellana, *L'Osservatore Romano*, 23 May 1988.

[9]Address at Fiorano, *L'Osservatore Romano*, 1 August 1988.

[10]*Christian Freedom and Liberation* §85 (page 17; Annex 2).

[11]Dignity is used in its prime meaning, viz. true worth, excellence.

[12]On the morally underdeveloped, see e.g. *Populorum Progressio*, (pages 89-90).

[13]On Conscience, see also §26, note 16 below, and page 102.

[14]For the kind of love meant, here and elsewhere in *Gaudium et Spes*, and in other documents, see pages 24-32.

[15]The Common Good: a similar definition is in §74 (not summarized) – "The common good embraces the sum total of all those conditions of social life which enable individuals, families and organizations to achieve complete and efficacious fulfilment."

[16]Conscience – the right to act according to a correct (or right) conscience: *"ius... ad agendum iuxta rectam suae conscientiae normam"*.

[17]See Genesis 1:26-28 (Annex 1); also Genesis 9:2-3 and Wisdom 9:2-3.

[18]On having and being, see also e.g. *Sollicitudo Rei Socialis* §28 (page 167 and the Index).

[19]Love: see pages 24-32.

[20]Phrase from the New Testament's Letter to the Hebrews (13:14).

[21]See the Gospel according to Matthew (23:3-33) and according to Mark (7:10-13). These record Christ's warnings to the falsely religious of his day. See also Jesus' words quoted in the last paragraph of *Gaudium et Spes:* "Not every one who says, 'Lord, Lord,' will enter the Kingdom of Heaven, but those who *do* the will of the Father" (Matthew 7:21 quoted in §93 on page 79).

[22]Christ, craftsman: see also page 29-30.

[23]Culture: see Note 3 above.

[24]The Second Vatican Council makes the points given here, in the chapter of *Gaudium et Spes* concerned with marriage and the family. Except for the points given, this chapter is one of those not included in the present summary. For further references to education see the Index.

[25]But the Church's doctrine is not a "third way" between capitalism and collectivism, nor is it an ideology: *Sollicitudo Rei Socialis* §41 (page 170).

[26]See *Laborem Exercens* (page 129) for extended consideration of work.

[27]Duty to ensure opportunity to work: see also pages 68-69.

[28]For a statement prepared by the Working Party on Human Rights established by the Bishops' Conference of England and Wales, see *The Right to Strike* (Annex 2).

[29]We should, indeed, share and employ our assets to help others. On Sharing, see also *Rerum Novarum* §19 and note 7 (pages 37, 40).

[30]In our private and family investing, for example; and in our business or trade union work, through any part we may have, alone or with colleagues, in matters of investment, plough-back, or training.

[31]See also §42 of *Sollicitudo Rei Socialis* (page 170). "Private property is under a social mortgage..."

[32]The beatitudes are the blessings Christ gave in his Sermon on the Mount (see Annex 1). For examples of the way the spirit of poverty can work, see *Apostolicam Actuositatem* §4 (page 83).

[33]Culture: see Note 3 above.

[34]Intermediary Bodies: see *Mater et Magistra* §59-67 (page 52); also page 18.

APOSTOLICAM ACTUOSITATEM

The Mission of Lay Christians

1965

Decree of the Second Vatican Council

The Latin title of this Decree is a polysyllabic plethora: a mouthful.

A further difficulty is to know what to call this document in English. Catholics usually call it The Laity Decree. In Church language "the laity" or "lay Christians" means Christians who are not priests, monks, nuns or the like. Though perhaps unfamiliar, the words laity and lay are probably the best we can do. At least they are short.

An alternative English title introduces a further unfamiliar word – polysyllabic, again: Decree on the *Apostolate* of Lay People. For apostolate, I have substituted Mission, to give the following as a full English title: The Mission of Lay Christians. For apostolate in most places in the text, I have substituted mission, role, or work. To have a short English title, we can adopt Laity Decree.

The Laity Decree affirms truths that *Gaudium et Spes* proposes to all humankind, and emphasizes their importance for lay Christians in particular. The Decree affirms justice, love and responsibility as keys to earthly development and human fulfilment in accord with God's design, and it affirms the role of the individual (§§8-19). The Decree stresses the need for training, and points to some of the means (§§30-32).

Readers of *Gaudium et Spes* know that the Catholic Church respects the worth of every human being. Readers of the Laity Decree will know that within her own immediate family the Church respects the worth of every member, of every lay member no less than every priest, monk and nun.

The reader may also note in paragraphs 3 and 4 the Council's mention of that special source of nourishment and refreshment for the Christian life, offered alike to laity, priests, monks and nuns: the Mass.

APOSTOLICAM ACTUOSITATEM

Sharing Christ's work

§2.   Lay Christians share in Christ's work, when for example we try to show the Gospel spirit in daily life.

§3.   To every lay Christian, in the Mass above all, the Holy Spirit offers the strength of love. He also offers talents for doing Christ's work in the world. Every lay Christian has the right and duty, for everyone's good, to develop and use these talents – including the most everyday ones.

Christian faith: daily life

§4.   Christian living is sustained by the spiritual helps available in the Church, and chiefly by active participation in the Mass.[1] Christians should make such use of these that, meeting our human obligations in the ordinary conditions of life, we do not separate our friendship with Christ from our ordinary work, but actually foster it there.

Family cares should not be foreign to our Christianness, nor should any other earthly interest. The love the Holy Spirit offers in our hearts can enable us to express the spirit of the beatitudes, concretely in our lives: we need feel no depression in want, no pride in plenty, no greed for vain show; we can be ready to accept loss and suffering to help other people.[2]

Christians should highly value competence in our ordinary job; also family and civic sense, honesty, sense of justice, sincerity, courtesy, and moral courage.

§5.   The lay Christian, at the same time a believer and a citizen of the world, has only a single conscience, a Christian conscience: it is this that must guide, in both domains.

Scale of values

§7.   Personal and family values, culture,[3] economic interests, the trades and professions, and their gradual development: all these are helps to human destiny, and also possess a
value of their own, placed in them by God. The goodness in
their nature receives added dignity from their relation with the
human person, for whose use they have been created.

In the course of history the use of earthly things has been
tarnished by serious defects. We have fallen into many errors
about God, human nature, and morality. And in modern times
some of us have put an immoderate trust in science and technology and have turned off into a kind of idolatry of the earthly.

It is the work of the entire Church – lay Christians as well
as priests and those in religious orders – to fashion men and
women able to establish the proper scale of values. A distinc-
tive task of lay Christians is this renewal of the earthly order.
Guided by the Gospel and the mind of the Church, prompted
by Christian love, lay Christians should act in this domain in
a direct way, in our own manner.

As citizens among citizens we must bring competence to
our cooperation with others, and act on our own responsibility. Everywhere and always we must seek the justice of the
Kingdom of God.

Justice and love

§8.   The greatest commandment is to love God and neighbour.
Lay Christians should support private and public help to the
poor, the sick, and all in need at home and abroad. Whenever
men and women lack the means for truly human life – food
and drink, clothes, housing, medicine, education, work –
Christians should go in search of them, find them out, and
help them. This obligation binds first and foremost the more
affluent individuals and nations.

The liberty and dignity of those helped must be respected.

We must first of all satisfy the demands of justice. "What
is already due in justice is not to be offered as a gift of charity."

We should remove the cause of evils, not just the effects.

We should help those in need gradually to become self-supporting.

Responsibility

§13.   Seeking to infuse the Christian spirit into the mentality, behaviour, laws and structures of the community is the special work and responsibility of lay Christians. It is at daily work where we are best qualified to help our fellows; and in our student days, at home, and locally.

Lay Christians accomplish the mission of Jesus' Church if we blend conduct and faith so as to be a light in the world; if we are upright in all dealings; if in love we share the living conditions, labours, sufferings and yearnings of other people; if we are aware of personal responsibility in the development of society, driving us on to fulfil family, social and working duties with Christian generosity. We should be good neighbours to everyone, spiritually and materially.

§.4.   In one or more of the ways open, lay Christians should participate in work for the common good at home and abroad through politics and public and social institutions.

The individual, alone and with others

§16.   In Christ's work in the world, the role of the individual is the starting point and key.

Every lay Christian has a call and duty to fulfil this role, even if there is no possibility of working with others: by the witness of a life of faith, trust and love; by explaining Christian teaching; by cooperating as citizens in everything to do with earthly affairs, seeking and showing the better motives of our behaviour; by worship, prayer and penance; by the willing acceptance of the labour and hardships of life.

§§18, 19 (24).   Since human beings are social by nature, lay Christians must also work together, for Christ: in families, parishes and dioceses for example. As long as a proper relationship is kept with Church authority, lay Christians have the right also to found and run associations, and to join those already existing. Often only concerted action can achieve full results.

First among associations to be supported are those that promote unity between faith and everyday life.

§27.   Catholics as individuals, and in Church groups, should cooperate with other Christians and with non-Christians who acknowledge human values, whenever Christian example indicates.

Training

§30.   Training for Christ's work should begin at the start of a child's education and continue through adolescence, youth and the whole of life. Parents should prepare their children – by example, above all – to recognize God's love and to have concern for neighbours' needs, material and spiritual. The family should become a kind of apprenticeship in Christ's work within the family and beyond.

Schools, colleges, lay groups and associations, and priests, also have responsibilities for this training. Training should take account of the entire range of Christians' work for Christ, especially in the sectors of working and social life.

Every lay Christian should also undertake her or his own preparation – adults especially, for as the years pass, self-awareness expands and allows us to get a clearer view of the talents God has given us, and to bring in better results from use of them for the good of other people.

§§31, 32.   Lay Christians should study the Church's doc-trine – her social teaching in particular – and should confront materialism with the witness of a Christian life. Means of study are available, from books and periodicals to conferences, retreats, study sessions and college courses.[4]

Call

§33.   The call of Christ and the Holy Spirit for helpers in God's work is made to all lay Christians; and in a special way to the younger generation.

NOTES
[Page numbers refer to pages in this book]

[1]See also *Gaudium et Spes* §§37-39 (page 73 above).

[2]The beatitudes are the blessings Christ gave in his Sermon on the Mount (see Annex1).

[3]Culture: see Note 3 to *Gaudium et Spes* (page 79).

[4]Plater College, Oxford, is prominent among institutions in Britain that offer study of the Church's social doctrine. Plater accepts students of every background and welcomes those who have not had opportunity for higher education before. Plater is sometimes called "The Second-Chance College". See also page 199.

POPULORUM PROGRESSIO

The Development of Peoples

1967

Encyclical Letter of Pope Paul VI

The chief concern of Pope Paul VI in this encyclical is for the poor of the materially under-developed nations of the world.

Popes before Paul VI knew the poor. Many popes came from poor families and poor places. As priests and as bishops, many lived and worked most of their lives in the world's poorer countries or districts. Once elected to the papacy, however, the nineteenth and twentieth century predecessors of Paul VI seldom left Italy.

The experience of Giovanni Battista Montini was different. Born in 1897 into a relatively prosperous family active in politics, publishing and the professions, he worked most of his adult life in the Vatican Secretariat of State. In 1954, nearing sixty, Monsignor Montini was made Archbishop of Milan, a city which had recovered fast from war. The Archbishop's interest in the Church's social doctrine, at the time of this energetic European renewal, may be seen in *Il Cristiano e il Benessere Temporale,*[1] which he wrote when at Milan.

In the nineteen fifties, for the first time in history, jet-fast long-distance travel became available. Archbishop Montini took advantage of it. He visited Latin America in 1960 and Africa in 1962. Elected Pope in 1963 after the death of John XXIII and taking the name Paul VI, he visited the Middle East and India, and Latin America a second time. For this man, life after sixty years in Europe had changed, in more ways than one.

What Paul VI saw and learned on his travels moved him deeply, and sharpened the interest he already had in the church's social doctrine. Whence his chief concern in *Populorum Progressio*, which he ends with the words, "Yes, We ask you, all of you, to heed Our cry of anguish, in the name of the Lord".

So great is the poverty of so many, in the materially under-developed world revealed to Archbishop and Pope, so heavy are the problems, that Paul VI devotes much of his encyclical to calls for concerted action at national and international levels. Also, however, he points to opportunities for action by individuals, working alone and together: these are the passages summarized below.

The reader will have noticed the word "materially" used in this introduction in front of the word "underdeveloped". Pope Paul reminds us that countries poor in food, housing, money, production and technology are not always poor in human qualities and assets; that they have things to teach as well as things to learn.[2] Pope John XXIII did the same: the materially underdeveloped countries "have often preserved acute awareness of the more important human values".[3] So did the Council: "People poor in material goods can be richer in wisdom".[4]

Pope Paul VI also reminds us of the other side of the coin. In rich countries, we can fall into materialism and greed, showing ourselves underdeveloped too, though in a different way: "Both for nations and for individuals, avarice is the most evident form of *moral* underdevelopment."[5] Is there moral underdevelopment in Britain?

POPULORUM PROGRESSIO

Development

§14.   Development cannot be limited to mere economic growth. To be authentic, development must be complete, integral; it has to promote the good of every person and of the whole person. The Church does not believe in separating the economic from the human.

§§15-17.   In the design of God, every one of us is called to develop and fulfil ourself. Every life is a vocation. "Endowed with intelligence and freedom, we are responsible for our fulfilment as we are for our salvation."

We are aided or impeded by those who educate us and
those with whom we live, but each of us remains the principal
agent of our own success or failure. Each of us can grow in
humanity, can enhance our personal worth, can become more
a person. And in union with Christ we can find still further
fulfilment: the greatest personal development, a transcendent
humanism.

Fullness of development is for ourself, and for all. It is
personal and communal.

Moral underdevelopment

§18.   This development would be threatened if the true scale
of values were undermined. The acquiring of possessions can
lead to greed, to insatiable desire for more. Individuals, families and nations can fall victim to stifling materialism.

§19.   Economic growth is essential if we are to develop as
human beings, but in a way it imprisons us if we consider it the
supreme good. It restricts our vision. Hearts harden, minds
close. Pursuit of possessions can distract us from individual
fulfilment. For nations and for individuals, avarice is the most
evident form of moral underdevelopment.

A new and complete humanism

§§20-21, 42.   If we need technicians for development, even
more do we need thought, wisdom and a new humanism which
will help us find ourselves anew; even more do we need love
and friendship, prayer and contemplation. This is what will
permit the fullness of authentic development, material and
moral, cultural, social and spiritual.

We must aim at complete humanism: the fully-rounded
development of the whole person and of all people, a true
humanism open to the values of the spirit and to God who is
their source; a humanism conscious of the vocation that gives
human life its true meaning.

The universal purpose of created things

§§22-23. From the first page on, the Bible teaches that the whole of creation is for every human being, and that it is our responsibility to develop it. The Second Vatican Council recalled that we have the right to find in the world what is necessary for each one of us.[6] All other rights are subordinate, including the rights of property and commerce. We are not justified in keeping for our own exclusive use what we do not need, when other lack necessities.

Industrialization

§25. Industry is a necessity. It is also a sign of human development and self-development. By work and intelligence we gradually wrest nature's secrets from her and find better use for her riches. As we master ourselves we develop a taste for research and discovery, an ability to take calculated risk, a boldness in enterprise – and generosity, and a sense of responsibility.

§26. We must recognize the contribution of labour and industry to development. We must also recognize the abuses we commit and allow, the abuses of liberal capitalism unchecked: profit the key motive for economic progress, competition the supreme law, private ownership an absolute right without limits or social obligation.

Work

§§27-28. Whether artist or craftsman, whether engaged in management, industry or agriculture,[7] everyone who works is a creator, in a way completing God's own work. Through work we can also improve our economic capabilities, acquiring perseverance, skill, and a spirit of invention. We can develop professional awareness, sense of duty, and love of neighbour.

Reform

§32.   Everyone should join in reforms with generosity, particularly those whose education, position and opportunities give them wide scope.

§33.   Public authority programmes are necessary to encourage, coordinate and supplement the activity of individuals and intermediary bodies. The authorities responsible should associate private initiative and intermediary bodies with the public work.[8]

§34.   "Such programmes should reduce inequalities, fight discriminations, free man from various types of servitude and enable him to be the instrument of his own material betterment, of his moral progress and spiritual growth. To speak of development is in effect to show as much concern for social progress as for economic growth. It is not sufficient to increase overall wealth for it to be distributed equitably. It is not sufficient to promote technology to render the world a more human place in which to live."

"The mistakes of their predecessors should warn those on the road to development of the dangers to be avoided. Tomorrow's technocracy can beget evils no less formidable than those due to the liberalism of yesterday. Economics and technology have no meaning except from man whom they should serve. And man is only truly man in as far as, master of his own acts and judge of their worth, he is author of his own advancement, in keeping with the nature given him by his Creator..."

Education

§35.   "It can even be affirmed that economic growth depends in the very first place upon social progress: thus basic education is the primary object of any plan of development. Hunger for education is no less debasing than hunger for food. An illiterate is a person with an undernourished mind." Literacy is an instrument of personal, social and economic development.

Help to the developing countries

§47. Even all the private and public effort and generosity given to fighting the hunger and thirst that torment so much of the world cannot suffice. The struggle against hunger, thirst and poverty, though urgent and necessary, is not enough. It is a question rather of building a world where every person can live a fully human life; a world where freedom is not an empty word and where the poor man Lazarus can sit down at the same table with the rich man.[9]

"Let each one examine his conscience... Is he prepared to support out of his own pocket works and undertakings in favour of the most destitute? Is he ready to pay higher taxes so that the public authorities can intensify their efforts in favour of development? Is he ready to pay a higher price for imported goods so that the producer may be more justly rewarded? Or to leave his country, if necessary and if he is young, in order to assist in the development of the young nations?"

§48 (67). In every nation we must produce goods to offer all our own people a truly human standard of living, and also to contribute to the development of the human race. We should consider it normal to devote part of production to meet the needs of the developing countries; to offer our knowledge and skill by working in them; to provide training; and to give hospitality to students.

§§59-61. Contract negotiators should remember the teaching of *Rerum Novarum*, always valid: if the positions of the contracting parties are too unequal, their consent does not suffice to guarantee justice, and the rule of free agreement remains subject to the natural law.[10] What is true of the just wage for the individual is also true of international contracts: an economy of exchange can no longer be based solely on free competition. Freedom of trade is fair only if it is subject to social justice.

§§70-72. If business takes us to the developing countries, we may be able to initiate social progress. Our sense of organization should suggest means for making intelligent use of the country's labour, for training, for giving scope for initiative and promotion, for preparing local people to share responsibilities and management.

If sent as an expert we should behave as helper and collaborator, not as overlord. People quickly perceive whether those who come are with or without affection, whether they come merely to apply their techniques or to recognize in people their full value.

The expert's civilization has no monopoly of valuable elements. We should be open to the history and culture of the host-country.

§74.   May all those who wish to belong to Christ hear his words: "I was hungry and you gave me food, I was thirsty and you gave me drink, I was a stranger and you made me welcome, lacking clothes and you clothed me, sick and you visited me..."[11]

§75.   Prayer should be matched by the resolute commitment of each individual to the struggle against underdevelopment.

§81.   Catholics in the more favoured nations should bring their talents and participation to development organizations, official or private, civil or religious.

Media, teaching

§83.   Teachers should awaken love for the peoples who live in misery. Those who work in the media can place before our eyes the efforts to promote development, and the sufferings we tend to forget, to spare our consciences.

Appeal

§§86-87.   All of you who work to answer the cries of the suffering – "You are the apostles of a development which is good and genuine, which is not wealth that is self-centred and sought for its own sake, but rather an economy at the service of man... With a full heart We bless you, and We appeal to all people of good will to join you... For, if the new name for peace is development, who would not wish to labour for it with all his powers? Yes, We ask you, all of you, to heed Our cry of anguish, in the name of the Lord."

NOTES
[Page numbers refer to pages in this book]

[1] An English edition was published in 1963 under the title *The Christian in the Material World* (The Christian and Prosperity would be nearer the original Italian). See Annex 2.

[2] §72 (page 94).

[3] *Mater et Magistra* §176 (page 57).

[4] *Gaudium et Spes* §15 (page 69).

[5] Moral Underdevelopment §§18 and 19 (page 90).

[6] *Gaudium et Spes* §69 (page 78).

[7] "or working at sea" – these words could well have been added. The principles taught by the Church apply for those who work on or under the sea no less than to those who work on or under the land, though landlubber popes do not always remember to say so.

[8] This reminder to Authority stems from the principle of Subsidiarity: (pages 20-21, 45). Intermediary bodies: see *Mater et Magistra* §§59-67 and note 12 (pages 52, 60).

[9] Luke 16:19-31 (see Annex 1).

[10] See page 38.

[11] Matthew 25:34-36 (see Annex 1).

MORAL QUESTIONS

1971

Statement of the Catholic Bishops' Conference of England and Wales

This Statement is one of the few relevant to our subject, issued by bishops of our own islands, in this instance the bishops of England and Wales. (The bishops of Scotland and the bishops of Ireland have independent organizations.) The Statement was a response to pressure from English and Welsh Catholics who were anxious or alarmed by the changes in Britain in the nineteen sixties and by the changes in the Church following the Second Vatican Council.

The Statement is compact. In its twenty-one pages it covers thirteen questions: The Christian Life, Civil Law and Morals, Race Relations, Justice in Industry, Social Justice at Home and Abroad, Civil Violence, War, Peace, Abortion, Death, Truth and Escapism, Marriage and Sexual Morality, Conscience and Church Teaching. It is written in brisk English. In its opening paragraphs there is even a tang of wit.

After the Vatican's brews – powerful, long-matured, sustaining, and true, but sometimes perhaps just a little heavy – this British gin and tonic is refreshing. In tasting it, remember that it was mixed for its times and circumstances.

The tastes that now follow are extracts, not summaries.

MORAL QUESTIONS

From the Bishops' Preface

§1. "The bishops are constantly being pressed to 'make a stand' or 'give a lead' on a multitude of moral questions. Many persons are alarmed at the reversal of traditional moral standards or at least bewildered by the changing moral climate of the day. They hope that the decline, as they see it, can be arrested by a firm affirmation of principles which they themselves hold firmly as the rule of life given by God to man...

§4. "The bishops of England and Wales some months ago invited the Catholic community to make known to them their opinion as to whether a statement would be useful and on what subjects. Many societies and individuals answered this request, sometimes in considerable detail. It should be clearly understood that the bishops were not asking for a plebiscite to decide on what is right and what is wrong. They were not asking for a vote on the revision of the Ten Commandments. They considered it right, however, to invite the people to say what in their judgement were the chief subjects on which a plain restatement of Christian moral teaching would be helpful at the present time.

"In the light of this enquiry and their own judgement the bishops now present this statement..."

The Christian life

§8. "Our model and our teacher is Christ our Lord. The law which he gave us is the law of love. 'You must love the Lord your God with all your heart, with all your soul, with all your mind and with all your strength... You must love your neighbour as yourself. There is no Commandment greater than these'."[1]

§9. "This is not a new teaching. He was quoting the law given by God in the Old Testament.[2] Moreover, it is a law which very many, besides Christians and Jews, have recognized as the ideal of human conduct at its highest. It is in the detailed application of this law to life that the Christian must be an example to the world. It is the Christian's duty to build up the Kingdom of God in this world in preparation for the perfect realization of that Kingdom in eternity. The Christian life must be lived in the light of eternity."

§10. "This is no abstract piece of unattainable idealism. Christ applied it with such realism that in the circumstances of the world we know it appears almost paradoxical. 'Do not be anxious, saying, "What shall we eat?" or "What shall we drink?" or "What shall we wear?"… your heavenly Father knows you need them all. But seek first his kingdom and his saving justice, and all these things shall be yours as well."[3]

§11.   "Christ does not exclude ordinary human prudence or the duty of men to provide for their families. He is giving us an attitude of mind. He put the same thing in other words when he said, 'No man can serve two masters; you cannot serve God and money'.[4] In the light of this, consider what has come to be called today the 'rat-race' – the determination to achieve power and wealth no matter who is trampled down in the process."

§12.   "The Christian's love of God is tested by his love for his neighbour. St John puts it: 'He who does not love his brother whom he has seen, cannot love God whom he has not seen'.[5] The parable of the Good Samaritan shows that the word 'neighbour' extends to all. The Christian must have care for all."

§13.   "Moreover, the Christian will reverence and admire good wherever it is to be found. There are those who believe themselves to be without any religion at all who yet show in their lives the kind of unselfishness and dedication to their fellow men which Christ preached."

§14.   "To live as a Christian will never be easy. Experience shows that opposition must be expected. Christ himself said we must expect it, but he told us to take up the Cross[6] and, in spite of all, he promised joy. 'You will be sorrowful, but your sorrow will be turned into joy'."[7]

§15.   "In short, the Christian life as described and exemplified by Christ himself is generous, courageous and loving. Christian morality will commend itself to others in so far as Christians live up to it. We shall raise the standards of morality in our society only by the example of our own lives."

§16. "Christ's words again are apposite: 'Your light must shine in people's sight, so that, seeing your good works, they may give praise to your Father in heaven'⁸..."

Justice in industry

§27. "...In commerce and industry the relation between employer and employee is not purely economic. A man's work is not a commodity to be bought or sold as the market price dictates. All work and production is primarily for the benefit of the whole community. All who work – at whatever level – have a stake in the community as persons, as sons of God, not as statistics. The first charge on industry should therefore be provision for the livelihood of those who are engaged in it. The criterion for wages and salaries should be the need for men to live as fully human persons, actual or prospective heads of families.

§28. "We recall too that Vatican II rejects 'every kind of discrimination which affects fundamental rights, whether it be social and cultural discrimination, or based on sex, race, colour, class, language or religion.'⁹

§29. "This does not mean a naïve disregard for efficiency and profitability. It does mean a proper regard for priorities. It is wrong that reorganization, automation, mergers and take-overs should be undertaken with a disregard for the persons employed..."

§30. "It would be too long to enter into a detailed examination of industrial relations. We recall simply that justice, charity and honesty are as much duties between groups as between individuals. For example, when the lowest paid workers negotiate a much-needed rise, the higher paid workers should think twice before urging their own claims. Charity and indeed social justice may well demand restraint here.

§31. "Irritation on the part of the public at inconvenient strikes in public services again needs to be tempered by a charitable understanding of what can be legitimate claims by the strikers. It still remains true that strikes and lockouts are a confession of failure. They mean that negotiation and discussion are replaced by a trial of strength. They are in fact a form of violence only to be justified as a last resort in a just cause. Christians should be ready to take an active part in their trade union or professional organization to work for justice and conciliation. Where understanding and patience are lacking on the part of management or labour, there can follow a disastrous succession of strikes which take the heart out of a man by destroying his pride and interest in the work he has to do.

§32.   "Honesty is the other virtue which needs emphasizing. It seems sometimes as though the larger the scale of financial affairs the less regard is had to honesty. A man who would be ashamed of petty pilfering finds his scruples progressively diminishing when it is a question of filling in time sheets, submitting expense accounts, negotiating a government contract. But 'Thou shalt not steal' applies at every level."

Social justice – home and abroad

§33.   "No community in the Church must be indifferent to those who are on its own doorstep. It should be a primary religious duty to discover and to help those who are in need within the boundaries of the parish. If this is done ecumenically, in collaboration with other Christians, so much the better. There is still real poverty in spite of all the social benefits that are provided. Nothing should take precedence over this work in any parish – neither social clubs nor religious sodalities. Lazarus[10] lies at the door; we must not ignore him.

§34.   "Social Justice concerns the whole community. Christians in this country, therefore, will be concerned for the developing countries, the 'Third World' as it is called. Nearly every comment submitted to the bishops called for this to be mentioned.

§35. "The need and our responsibility are obvious, the remedy sometimes obscured. As for the need, anyone who has travelled knows it well. The contrast between their poverty and our affluence is disturbing: we are Dives, they are Lazarus. We can find all kinds of excuses for doing nothing – the immensity of the need, the callousness of the wealthy in underdeveloped countries themselves. But no excuses will serve. We are Christians – Christ stands there before us and says, 'I was hungry and you never gave me food'.[11] This is one of the rare times when Our Lord warns us of eternal damnation. The Christian should not need the warning – enough that Christ in the person of our brethren is hungry. But the remedy? Many of these countries are potentially wealthy. But they need an 'assisted take-off', that is, they need to be given, not just lent, the means to begin their development. Evidently aid at national and international level is one requirement. Governments hesitate because they are only too aware of the constant claims of their own people for further social benefits, reduced taxes and the like. The Christian has to ask himself: 'Am I prepared to tell my government I am ready to forgo this or that benefit so that greater aid can be given to the Third World countries?'

§36. "The need for national action is no excuse for doing nothing personally. The modern call to aid the people of the Third World is really only one aspect of the age-old missionary effort of the Church for the material as well as the spiritual welfare of the peoples of developing countries. Every Catholic parish and family should therefore renew its sense of mission and increase support of the missionary organizations and particularly CAFOD, the central fund set up by the bishops called Catholic Aid for Overseas Development. We are no longer bound to Friday abstinence. But we are always bound to some equivalent form of self-sacrifice. What better than to feed the hungry, to clothe the naked, to help Christ suffering in our brothers and sisters?"

Conscience and Church teaching

§74. "This statement is obviously not a comprehensive guide to the Christian life. It has touched on matters which happen to be uppermost in the minds of Christians at the moment. There are many other urgent problems and their full solution is not always immediately clear. We should not expect to find answers ready made for every situation. In particular instances the Christian must make his own responsible judgement. The more his life is modelled on the life of Christ, the more likely he will be to make right judgements in the sight of God. Conscience implies the making of such a judgement. Like every other judgement, its correctness will depend on the information on which it is based and the objectivity with which it is made. It is our duty to follow conscience but it is equally our duty to make sure that conscience has the necessary information to guide us. That is what we mean by an informed conscience. A false conscience will lead us astray.

§75. "What information has a man to go on when making a conscientious decision?
First: the example of Christ, the principles he gave, the life he led.
Second: the experience of the Christian community from the time of Christ to the present day. We believe Christ is with his Church and never ceases to guide and enlighten it.
Third: the guidance and authoritative teaching of the successors of the Apostles and especially of Peter.

§76. "Insight into the teaching of Christ grows throughout time as the members of his Church live the Christian life. We call this the development of doctrine. It is clear that human intelligence will start to work on any body of truth it receives, comparing, deducing, speculating, probing deeper and deeper. God gave us our intelligence. He gave us his revelation in Christ. It is God's will we should explore and develop it.

§77. "But how can we guarantee that our conclusions are truly a development and not a distortion? Precisely to safeguard against distortion Christ gave particular teaching authority to his Apostles, to Peter and their successors: 'He that heareth you heareth me'; 'Feed my lambs, feed my sheep'; 'Whatsoever you shall bind on earth shall be bound in Heaven'; 'Go, teach all nations... I am with you all days, even to the consummation of the world'. These words cannot be ignored.

§78. "Now the Church takes great care not to extend the meaning of Christ's words further than they warrant. Evidently he gives special authority and special guidance to the Apostles and their successors. But the Church carefully observes the limits. So, granted that Christ will ensure they lead the Church aright, the least one can say is that the Pope, or the College of Bishops with the Pope their head, will infallibly be right when they solemnly define and state a doctrine as being part of the teaching of the Church. Such statements are rare.

§79. "But the guidance given by the Pope and the bishops carries a particular weight and authority even when there is no question of an infallible statement. They are the successors of the Apostles and it was clearly the intention of Christ that they should give day to day guidance to his Church. St Paul, addressing the ones in charge of the Church at Ephesus, said: 'Take heed to yourselves and to all the flock, in which the Holy Spirit has made you guardians, to feed the Church of the Lord which he obtained with his own blood. I know that after my departure fierce wolves will come in among you, not sparing the flock; and from among your own selves will arise men speaking perverse things, to draw away the disciples after them. Therefore be alert...'[12]

§80. "It must be expected that the Pope and the bishops will have special graces and light to guide the Church. There will be naturally a wide range of degrees of authority in such teaching. The guidance of the Pope will carry vastly more weight than that of any individual bishop. But in any case the guidance cannot simply be dismissed or ignored on the grounds that it is not, in a particular instance, an infallible definition.

§81. "In short, a conscientious judgement must be conscientiously made taking into account all the guidance which

Christ has given us. We must remember that judgement can be warped by ignorance, haste, fear and other factors. In making a decision we are less likely to choose a course that involves difficulty or hardship for ourselves or others. The responsibility for a wrong judgement in such cases would evidently vary. It must be remembered that Christ told us to expect hardship and even death. He did not tell us to slip away from them. He promised to help us to persevere in spite of them. Circumstances may modify responsibility. They cannot make wrong right and right wrong.

§82.   "Ultimately, our life will be a success in the eyes of God the more we grow like Christ our Lord. Do we seriously fulfil in our life the picture Christ gave of the citizen of his Kingdom – poor in spirit, meek, hungering and thirsting for holiness, merciful, clean of heart, peacemaker, suffering persecution for holiness' sake?[13] Our moral judgement will be likely to be right the more our moral development follows that pattern. Who will dare to say he has attained it? The best we can hope to say is 'God have mercy on me a sinner'.[14] Prayer and the grace of God which follows it will be our strength. Christ did not simply give a command to lead the kind of life summarized in the Sermon on the Mount. He promised to live our lives with us. 'I am the way, the truth and the life'.[15] 'I am come that they may have life and have it more abundantly'."[16]

NOTES
[Page numbers refer to pages in this book]

[1]Mark 12:28-31: the Great Commandments (see Annex 1).
[2]Deuteronomy 6:4 and Leviticus 19:18.
[3]Matthew 6:31-33.
[4]Matthew 6:24.
[5]1 John 4:20.
[6]Matthew 16:24.
[7]John 16:20.
[8]Matthew 5:16.
[9]*Gaudium et Spes* §29 (page 71).
[10]Luke 16:19-31 (see Annex 1).

[11]Matthew 25:42: from the Last Judgement (see Annex 1).
[12]Acts 20:28-31.
[13]Matthew 5: the Beatitudes (see Annex 1).
[14]Luke 18:13.
[15]John 14:6.
[16]John 10:10.

OCTOGESIMA ADVENIENS

Eightieth Anniversary

1971

Apostolic Letter[1] of Pope Paul VI

Some of the matters to which Pope Paul VI drew attention on the eightieth anniversary of *Rerum Novarum* might be thought purely social. Certainly Pope Paul's concern for the materially underdeveloped countries is again clear. There is also, however, relevance to our economic life in Britain.

After a paragraph of his Foreword on the Church's social doctrine, the Pope in his Chapter I considers among other things urbanization[2] – a word as wretched as urban life itself can but need not be. He refers to "a new loneliness"; to new proletariats – people who have no ownership; to discrimination, indifference and delinquency; to the demoralization of men and women waiting in vain for a decent dwelling at a price they can afford.

The eleven pages of Pope Paul's Chapter II consider Christianity in relation to ideologies, to philosophical teachings, historical movements and -isms such as Marxism, socialism, atheistic materialism, liberalism, utopianism; in relation to the human sciences and the notion of progress. Chapter III looks at economic and political power, with emphasis on justice and the common good, and on the attainment of our true and complete good. It reminds political power of the doctrine of subsidiarity[3] and considers the sharing of responsibility in matters social and political as well as economic. Two chapters worth reading, though they cannot be given much space in the present work.

The Letter ends with a fresh and insistent reminder that every Christian has personal responsibility in the community.

OCTOGESIMA ADVENIENS

The social teaching and its application

§4.   It is up to Christians to analyze with objectivity the situation proper to their own country in the light of the Gospel, and "to draw principles of reflection, criteria for judgement, and directives for action, from the social teaching of the Church". It is up to Christians, with the help of the Holy Spirit, with their bishops, with those from different Christian communities and with all men and women of goodwill, to discern the options and commitments called for.

Urbanization

§§10-12.   "Man is experiencing a new loneliness, not in the face of a hostile nature which it has taken him centuries to subdue, but in an anonymous crowd in which he feels himself a stranger." New proletariats – the new propertyless – install themselves in decayed districts or in "belts of misery besieging in a still silent protest the luxury which blatantly cries out from the centres of consumption and waste".

Cities can foster discrimination, indifference, exploitation, delinquency, and the demoralization of men and women waiting in vain for a decent dwelling at a price they can afford. We need to create new modes of neighbourliness, to accept new responsibility.[4]

Trade unions

§14.   The role of unions is important. Through unions we can collaborate in economic advance and develop responsibility for the common good.[5]

As a final means of defence, the right to strike remains certainly recognised; but we should not use strength to impose by strike conditions too burdensome for the economy, or demands directly political. When it is a question of services required for the life of an entire nation, we must assess the limit beyond which the harm caused becomes inadmissible.[6]

Discernment

§§15-16. Tempted by egoism and domination as we always are, we need discernment to root out new injustices. Christians must defend and help the new poor: the handicapped, the old, those on the fringe, and others at disadvantage in times of industrial change or in a society hardened by competition and success.

We should admit all citizens to economic, cultural, civic and social life and to fair shares in the nation's riches, without discrimination on account of race, origin, colour, culture, sex or religion.

Social innovation

§19. "In no other age have we been so explicitly called to social innovation. To this we should devote resources of invention and capital as important as those invested for armaments or technology."

Responsibility in the media

§20. Those of us with power in the media have a grave moral responsibility for truth, for the needs and reactions we generate and the values we put forward.

Equality and participation: love

§§22-23. Two aspirations in our new world of science and technology are equality and participation, two forms of human dignity and freedom. Legislation is necessary for achieving these aspirations, but legislation is not sufficient. Love is needed as well: preferential respect for the poor, for example.

Those of us who are more fortunate should renounce some of our rights so as to place our goods more generously at the service of others.

If, beyond legal rules, we have no deeper feeling of respect for and service to others, then even equality before the law can be an alibi for discrimination, exploitation and contempt. Without education in solidarity, equality overemphasized can give rise to an individualism in which each of us claims our own rights without wishing to be answerable for the common good.

The Christian spirit has a contribution to make. Love for man is "the prime value of the earthly order".

Progress

§41. "...What is the meaning of this never-ending, breathless pursuit of a progress that eludes us just when we believe we have conquered it and can enjoy it in peace?" We justly condemn merely quantitative economic growth: we want the qualitative also. "The quality and truth of human relations; participation and responsibility: these are no less important for our future than the quantity and variety of goods produced and consumed."

The social doctrine

§42. The Church's teaching accompanies us on our search for answers to the new questions we face. It develops through reflection applied to our changing situations, under the force of the Gospel, with impartial will to serve, and with attention to the poorest.

§45. Human beings yearn for freedom from need and dependence. This liberation starts with the interior freedom we must find again with regard to our goods and our powers; we will never reach it except through love for humanity, and readiness to serve. Otherwise revolutionary ideologies lead only to a change of masters.

Responsibility

§47. "...In *Mater et Magistra* Pope John XXIII stressed how much the admittance to responsibility is a basic demand of human nature, an exercise of freedom and a path to human development. He showed how, in economic life and particularly in enterprise, this sharing in responsibilities should be ensured. Today the field is wider, and extends to the social and political sphere... To counterbalance increasing technocracy, we must devise modern forms of democracy, not only making it possible for each person to become informed and to express himself or herself, but also by involving each person in a shared responsibility..."

§48. "Let every Christian examine himself, to see what he has done up to now, and what he ought to do. It is not enough to recall principles, state intentions, point to injustices...; these words will lack weight unless they are accompanied for each individual by a livelier awareness of personal responsibility and by effective action. It is too easy to throw back on others responsibility for injustices, if we do not realize how each one shares in it personally, and how personal conversion[7] is needed first."

NOTES
[Page numbers refer to pages in this book]

[1]Apostolic letter: a Letter addressed to a particular person or group rather than to many. *Octogesima Adveniens* is addressed to Maurice Cardinal Roy, in 1971 President of the Council of the Laity and of the Commission for Justice and Peace.

[2]Urbanization: §§10-12, (page 107).

[3]§46 (not summarized). On Subsidiarity, see pages 20-21, 45.

[4]See also *Gaudium et Spes:* §24-32 (pages 70-72) *Homeless:* see pages 162-164

[5]See also *Gaudium et Spes* (page77).

[6]On strikes, see also *Gaudium et Spes*§68 and Note [28] pages 77 and 80).

[7]Conversion: described by Paul VI in *Evangelii Nuntiandi* §§8-10 (page 114) as "a profound change of mind and heart" and by John Paul II in *Sollicitudo Rei Socialis* §§35-38 (pages 168-169) as "change in mentality and way of living". See also *Apostolicam Actuositatem* §§7-19 (pages 84-85).

JUSTICE IN THE WORLD

1971

Document of the Synod of Bishops in Rome

One of the results of the Second Vatican Council has been a series of synods of bishops held in Rome. The third synod met in the autumn of 1971, for work on priesthood and on justice.

Present injustice and future danger, in the contrasts between the materially advanced and the materially underdeveloped countries, were a prominent concern the world over in the years that led to this synod. In the Catholic Church, the concern had been heard in the words of popes, Council, national bishops and laity. The same concern was prominent in the Roman synod.

In the document the bishops issued on justice, they gave most attention to analysis and commentary on the signs of the times, to principles, to issues special to the underdeveloped countries, and to action at national and international levels. Some of the relatively few paragraphs pertinent to individual responsibility in the advanced countries are summarized below.

JUSTICE IN THE WORLD

Resources

§§11-12. Sources of food, fuel for warmth, and elements as necessary as air and water could all be threatened unless we change the model of high and ever-increasing consumption and pollution which in the materially advanced countries we have given to the world. A merely economic progress is insufficient for human dignity.

§48. Those of us who are Christians must ask ourselves whether our lifestyle gives a good example of the restraint in consumption which we preach to others.

Love and justice

§34.   Our response to God's love shows in our love and service of other people. Christian love demands justice: a recognition of the dignity and rights of one's neighbour.

§38.   We all have the right and duty to promote the common good. In all aspects of our life, including family and work, those of us who are Christians, especially, should fulfil our responsibilities with fidelity and with competence, as a leaven in society, guided by the gospel and the Church but normally acting on our own initiative.

Education

§49.   In everyday life – in the family, at work, in social and civic life, and in education – we have opportunity to apply an understanding of the gospel. In education – at home and at school – we can help show how a full life can be lived in accord with morality both personal and social.

§50.   In our work in education, and in the media, we have sometimes encouraged an individualism that is narrow, and a mentality that exalts possessions. We sometimes try to help our young to grow up only as society wishes them to be, produced in society's own image, copies of ourselves as we are, instead of the new person of the gospel.

§51.   Our work in education demands a renewal of heart, and a recognition of sin both individual and social. It should prepare people for a way of life that is genuinely and fully human, in justice, love, and simplicity. It should awaken a critical sense, and lead us to reflect on society and its values. It should help us resist manipulation by the media or by political power.

§53.   Education does not end for us, at any age; and it must also have its practical side, getting us involved in what is going on, and into direct contact with injustices.

§§54-55.   Education for justice starts in the family, in learning respect for other human beings.

The Mass

§58.   At the heart of the Church's life, the Mass can greatly serve education for justice. The Mass gives us the Church's teaching, and Christ's example. It can help us to thankfulness for our blessings and to awareness of the needs of others. It can nourish conscience. It can inspire us to service, as individuals and as members of a community.

EVANGELII NUNTIANDI

Proclaiming the Gospel

1975

Apostolic Exhortation of Pope Paul VI

Encyclical letters, conciliar constitution and decree, bishops' statements, an apostolic letter – and now an apostolic exhortation: a type of document used by popes when building upon the work of synods of bishops.

The third synod issued its own document (see page 111). The fourth, held in 1974 to discuss the proclaiming of the Gospel in the modern world, remitted its work and proposals to Pope Paul VI, who in the following year issued *Evangelii Nuntiandi*. (The synods of 1980 and 1987 did likewise, resulting in *Familiaris Consortio* in 1981 and *Christifideles Laici* in 1988.)

Evangelii Nuntiandi, addressed to Catholics, contains little that deals expressly with the economy. It does however have the paragraphs summarized or quoted below.

EVANGELII NUNTIANDI

Change: the individual

§§8-10.   Christ proclaims two things: a kingdom, and salvation. The first is the kingdom of God, where we find happiness in things the world rejects. The second is liberation from everything that oppresses us – above all, from sin and evil.

God offers both things to every human being. At the same time, each individual must gain them through even the severest difficulties, through a life lived in accord with the Gospel – "But above all, each individual gains them through a total interior renewal..., a radical conversion, a profound change of mind and heart".

Development and liberation

§31. "Between evangelization and human advancement – development and liberation – there are profound links. These include links of an anthropological order, because the man who is to be evangelized is not an abstract being but is subject to social and economic questions. They also include links in the theological order, since one cannot dissociate the plan of Creation from the plan of Redemption. The latter plan touches the very concrete situations of injustice to be combatted and of justice to be restored. They include links of the eminently evangelical order, which is the order of love. How can one proclaim the new commandment without promoting in justice and peace the true, authentic advancement of man?"

§33. Liberation cannot be contained in the dimension of economics, politics, social or cultural life. It must envisage the whole person, in all our aspects, right up to and including our openness to the divine absolute. It is attached to a certain concept of man, which it can never sacrifice to any strategy, practice or short-term efficiency.

§34. "Hence when preaching liberation and associating herself with those who work and suffer for it, the Church is certainly not willing to restrict her mission to the religious field only and dissociate herself from man's temporal problems. Nevertheless she reaffirms the primacy of her spiritual vocation and refuses to replace the proclamation of the Kingdom by the proclamation of forms of human liberation. Her contribution to liberation is incomplete if she neglects to proclaim salvation in Jesus Christ."

§35. Not every notion of liberation is consistent with the Gospel's understanding of human beings; and for God's kingdom to come it is not enough to establish liberation and to create well-being and development.

Structures and systems: the individual

§36.   It is important for us to build structures which are more human, more just, more respectful of the rights of the person, less oppressive, less enslaving; but the best structures and systems soon become inhuman if the inhuman inclinations of the heart are not made wholesome, if those who live in the structures or who rule them do not undergo conversion of heart and outlook.

The Church's teaching

§38.   To encourage us, the Church offers the inspiration of faith, the motivation of love, and a social teaching which the true Christian cannot ignore and which he or she must make the foundation of wisdom and experience, and translate into action, participation and commitment.

Education

§78.   "Parents and teachers, your task – and the many conflicts of the present day do not make it easy – is to help your children and your students to discover truth, including religious and spiritual truth."

REDEMPTOR HOMINIS

Redeemer of Humankind

1979

Encyclical Letter of Pope John Paul II

Quarry worker, poet, linguist, philosopher, theologian, priest, student of humankind, and (even if Polish prolixity sometimes tries listener and reader) teacher *sans pareil.* Such is John Paul II. He was elected Pope in October 1978, following the death of Paul VI and the death of John Paul I after only thirty-three days in office.

Redemptor Hominis is John Paul II's first encyclical. Few of its ninety-eight pages refer expressly to economics, but some do, and – more important – much of the teaching of *Redemptor Hominis* applies to the economic departments of life as well as to others.

As the title indicates, the Letter looks at Christ's work in our world. The Letter also inaugurates a pontificate destined to serve more than ten of the last years leading to a new century and a new millenium. These are further reasons for not ignoring R*edemptor Hominis.*

Though reproducing with little change not the Pope's Polish or Latin but the Vatican's translation into English, the extracts which now follow may give the reader a scent of John Paul II's style.

REDEMPTOR HOMINIS

What modern man is afraid of

15.2[1]. "...The man of today seems ever to be under threat from what he produces, that is to say from the result of the work of his hands and, even more so, of the work of his intellect and the tendencies of his will. All too soon, and often in an unforeseeable way, what this manifold activity of man yields is not only subjected to 'alienation', in the sense that it is simply taken away from the person who produces it, but rather it turns against man himself, at least in part, through the indirect consequences of its effects returning on himself...; he is afraid that it can become the means and instrument for an unimaginable self-destruction, compared with which all the cataclysms and catastrophes of history known to us seem to fade away. This gives rise to a question: Why is it that the power given to man from the beginning by which he was to subdue the earth² turns against himself...?"

15.3.   "We seem to be increasingly aware of the fact that the exploitation of the earth, the planet on which we are living, demands rational and honest planning... Man often seems to see no other meaning in his natural environment than what serves for immediate use and consumption. Yet it was the Creator's will that man should communicate with nature as an intelligent and noble master and guardian, and not as a heedless exploiter and destroyer."

15.4.   "The development of technology and the development of contemporary civilization... demand a proportional development of morals and ethics. For the present, this last development seems to be always left behind. Accordingly, in spite of the marvel of this progress, in which it is difficult not to see also authentic signs of man's greatness... this progress cannot fail to give rise to disquiet on many counts. The first reason for disquiet concerns the essential and fundamental question: Does this progress... make human life on earth more human in every aspect of that life? Does it make it more worthy of man? There can be no doubt that in various aspects it does. But the question keeps coming back with regard to what is most essential – whether in the context of this progress man, as man, is becoming truly better, that is to say more mature spiritually, more aware of the dignity of his humanity, more responsible, more open to others, especially the neediest and the weakest, and readier to give, and to aid all."

15.5. "This question must be put by Christians, precisely because Jesus Christ has made them so universally sensitive about the problem of man... Do all the conquests attained until now and those projected for the future for technology accord with man's moral and spiritual progress? In this context is man, as man, developing and progressing or is he regressing and being degraded in his humanity? In men and in man's world, which in itself is a world of moral good and evil, does good prevail over evil? In men and among men is there a growth of social love, of respect for the rights of others – for every person, nation and people – or on the contrary is there an increase of various degrees of selfishness, exaggerated nationalism instead of authentic love of country, and also the propensity to dominate others beyond the limits of legitimate rights and merits and the propensity to exploit the whole of material progress and the technology of production for the purpose of dominating others or of favouring this or that imperialism?..."

Progress or threat

16.1. "If therefore our time... shows itself a time of great progress, it is also seen as a time of threat in many forms for man. The Church must speak of this threat to all people of goodwill and must always carry on a dialogue with them about it. Man's situation in the modern world seems indeed to be far removed from the objective demands of the moral order, from the requirements of justice, and even more of social love. We are dealing here only with that which found expression in the Creator's first message to man at the moment in which he was giving him the earth, to 'subdue it'.[3] This first message was confirmed by Christ the Lord in the mystery of the Redemption. This is expressed by the Second Vatican Council in these beautiful chapters of its teaching that concern man's 'kingship', that is to say his call to share in the kingly function of Christ himself.[4] The essential meaning of this 'kingship' and 'dominion' of man over the visible world, which the Creator himself gave man for his task, consists in the priority of ethics over technology, in the primacy of the person over things, and in the superiority of spirit over matter."

16.2. "This is why all phases of present-day progress must be followed attentively. Each stage of that progress must, so to speak, be x-rayed from this point of view. What is in question is the advancement of persons, not just the multiplying of things people can use. It is a matter – as a contemporary philosopher has said and as the Council has stated – not so much of 'having more' as of 'being more'.[5] Indeed there is already a real perceptible danger that, while man's dominion over the world of things is making enormous advances, he should lose the essential threads of his dominion and in various ways let his humanity be subjected to the world and become himself something subject to manipulation in many ways – even if the manipulation is often not perceptible directly – through the whole of the organization of community life, through the production system and through pressure from the means of social communication. Man cannot relinquish himself or the place in the visible world that belongs to him; he cannot become the slave of things, the slave of economic systems, the slave of production, the slave of his own products... It is not a matter here merely of giving an abstract answer to the question: Who is man? It is a matter of the whole of the dynamism of life and civilization. It is a matter of the meaningfulness of the various initiatives of everyday life, and also of the premises for many programmes – political programmes, economic ones, social ones, state ones, and others..."

16.3. "...Everyone is familiar with the picture of the consumer civilization, which consists in a surplus of goods necessary for man and for entire societies (we are dealing here with the rich highly developed societies) while the remaining societies (at least broad sectors of them) are suffering from hunger, with many people dying each day of starvation and malnutrition. Hand in hand go abuse of freedom by one group – an abuse linked precisely with a consumer attitude uncontrolled by ethics – and a limitation by it of the freedom of the others, that is to say those suffering marked shortages and being driven to conditions of even worse misery and destitution."

16.4. "This pattern and contrast represent the gigantic development of the parable in the Bible of the rich banqueter and the poor man Lazarus.[6] So widespread is the phenomenon that it brings into question the financial, monetary, production and commercial mechanisms which, resting on various political pressures, support the world economy... By submitting man to tensions created by himself, as at an accelerated pace we run down material and energy resources and compromise the geophysical environment, these structures unceasingly make the areas of misery spread, accompanied by anguish, frustration and bitterness."

16.5. "We have before us here a great drama that can leave nobody indifferent. The person who, on the one hand is trying to draw the maximum profit and on the other hand is paying the price in damage and injury, is always man. The drama is made still worse by the presence close at hand of the privileged social classes and of the rich countries, which accumulate goods to an excessive degree and the misuse of whose riches very often becomes the cause of various ills. Add to this the fever of inflation and the plague of unemployment – these are further symptoms of the moral disorder that is being noticed in the world situation and therefore requires daring creative resolves in keeping with man's authentic dignity."

16.6. "Such a task is not an impossible one. The principle of solidarity, in a wide sense, must inspire the effective search for appropriate institutions and mechanisms, whether in the sector of trade, where the laws of healthy competition must be allowed to lead the way, or on the level of a wider and more immediate redistribution of riches and of control over them, in order that the economically developing peoples may be able not only to satisfy their essential needs but also to advance gradually and effectively."

16.7. "This difficult road of the transformation of the structures of economic life is one on which it will not be easy to go forward without the intervention of a true conversion of mind, will and heart. The task requires resolute commitment by individuals and peoples who are free and linked in solidarity... Economic development, with every factor in its adequate functioning, must be constantly programmed and realized within a perspective of universal joint development of each individual and people, as was convincingly recalled by my predecessor Paul VI in *Populorum Progressio*. Otherwise, the category of 'economic progress' becomes in isolation a superior category subordinating the whole of human existence to its partial demands, suffocating man, breaking up society, and ending by entangling itself in its own tensions and excesses."

16.8. "It is possible to undertake this duty... One thing is certain: at the basis of this gigantic sector it is necessary to establish, accept and deepen the sense of moral responsibility, which man must undertake. Again and always man."

16.9. "This responsibility becomes especially evident for us Christians when we recall – and we should always recall it – the scene of the Last Judgement according to the words of Christ related in Matthew's Gospel."[7]

16.10. "This scene must always be applied to man's history; it must always be made the measure for human acts as an essential outline for an examination of conscience by each and every one: 'I was hungry and you gave me no food... naked and you did not clothe me... in prison and you did not visit me'. These words become charged with even stronger warning, when we think that, instead of bread and cultural aid, the new States and nations awakening to independent life are being offered, sometimes in abundance, modern weapons and means of destruction placed at the service of armed conflicts and wars that are not so much a requirement for defending their just rights and their sovereignty but rather a form of chauvinism, imperialism, and neocolonialism of one kind or another. We all know well that the areas of misery and hunger on our globe could have been made fertile in a short time, if the gigantic investments for armaments at the service of war and destruction had been changed into investments for food at the service of life."

16.11.   "...The Church, which has no weapons at her disposal apart from those of the spirit, of the word and of love, cannot renounce her proclamation of the word, in season and out of season. For this reason she does not cease to beg everybody in the name of God and in the name of man... Think of your brothers and sisters who are suffering hunger and misery! Respect each one's dignity and freedom!"

Kingly service

21.1.   "...Among the elements that stand out in the teaching of the Second Vatican Council is this: our sharing in Christ's kingly mission. That is to say, rediscovering in oneself and others the special dignity of our vocation that can be described as 'kingship'. This dignity is expressed in readiness to serve, in keeping with the example of Christ, who 'came not to be served but to serve'.[8] If, in the light of this attitude of Christ's, 'being a king' is truly possible only by 'being a servant', then 'being a servant' also demands so much spiritual maturity that it must really be described as 'being a king'.

21.2.   "For the whole of the community of the People of God and for each member of it what is in question is not just a social membership; rather, for each and every one, what is essential is a vocation... Membership has for its source a particular call, united with the saving action of grace. We must see first and foremost Christ saying in a way to each member of the community: 'Follow me'. It is the community of the disciples, each of whom in a different way – at times very consciously and consistently, at other times not very consciously and very inconsistently – is following Christ.[11]

21.3.   "Every initiative serves true renewal in the Church and helps to bring the authentic light that is Christ insofar as the initiative is based on adequate awareness of the individual Christian's vocation and responsibility... This principle, the key rule for the whole of Christian practice, must with due proportion be applied to the whole of humanity and to each human being... It is the basis on which their lives must be built by married people, parents, and women and men of different conditions and professions, from those who occupy the highest posts in society to those who perform the simplest tasks. It is precisely the principle of the 'kingly service' that imposes on each one of us, in imitation of Christ's example, the duty to demand of himself exactly what we have been called to, what we have personally obliged ourselves to by God's grace, in order to respond to our vocation..."

21.4.   "...Basing ourselves on Christ's example and collaborating with the grace that he has gained for us, we are able to attain to 'being kings', that is to say we are able to produce a mature humanity in each one of us. Mature humanity means full use of the gift of freedom received from the Creator when he called to existence the man made in his image, after his likeness..."

21.5.   "Nowadays it is sometimes held, wrongly, that freedom is an end in itself, that each human being is free when he makes use of freedom as he wishes, and that this must be our aim in the lives of individuals and societies. In reality, freedom is a great gift only when we know how to use it consciously for everything that is our true good. Christ teaches us that the best use of freedom is love, which takes concrete form in self-giving and in service..."

NOTES
[Page numbers refer to pages in this book]

[1]The English edition of *Redemptor Hominis* published by the Catholic Truth Society (see Annex 2) is arranged in long, numbered sections, each built of unnumbered paragraphs. The present extracts adopt the Section numbers, and after a decimal point add numbers for the paragraphs.

[2]Genesis 1:28 (see Annex 1).

[3]Genesis 1: (see Annex 1). 'Subdue' or 'conquer', according to translation.

[4]*Lumen Gentium* (not summarized in the present work) §§10, 36. See also *Redemptor Hominis* §21.

[5]*Gaudium et Spes* §35 (page 73). Also *Populorum Progressio* §14 (page 89); *Sollicitudo Rei Socialis* §28 (page 167).

[6]Luke 16:19-31 (see Annex 1).

[7]Matthew 25:31-46 (see Annex 1).

[8]Matthew 20:28 (see Annex 1). See also John 13:1-17.

THE EASTER PEOPLE

1980

Message from the Catholic Bishops of England and Wales

In Liverpool over a period of five days in May 1980 the Catholic bishops together with clergy, members of orders and societies, and lay men and women from every diocese met in a National Pastoral Congress, to share their thinking about the Christian life of the Catholic community in England and Wales.

In August the bishops issued a seventy-page Message entitled *The Easter People*, setting out their reflections on the work of the Congress. Extracts are given below.

"Many find the word 'holiness' off-putting", says the Message. It nonetheless notes the call to holiness in daily and working life made by Christ and his Church to every person, to lay men and women no less than to nuns, monks and priests. It also notes the stressing by Congress delegates of the need for holiness in their own lives, and in a section headed by the off-putting word the bishops suggest what this holiness is. Here is the Gospel and the Second Vatican Council, in language of British to British.

THE EASTER PEOPLE

The social doctrine

§162. "As bishops we should take urgent steps to encourage the study and development of the Church's social teaching, and to ensure that such teaching is treated as a priority in all programmes of adult education and formation. The social teachings of the Church must be recognized as an essential part of its doctrine and be presented in the upper forms of our secondary schools in a way which will instruct and inspire young people to assume their responsibilities in the community..."

Daily work

§163. "...Many practising Catholics are unused to making a conscious link between their faith and their daily work. But all men and women are called to labour with the talents they have been given to advance the coming of God's kingdom on earth and to help bring creation to fulfilment. Work can be a service to our fellow men..."

Resources and wealth

§166. "...We urge Catholics to work... for the transformation of whatever structures and institutions prevent people throughout the world from living fully human lives... We acknowledge the responsibility which rests with the people of God and with each individual to work for a more just distribution of the world's goods and resources, for more comprehensive programmes of sharing our wealth with others in greater need, and for the adoption by individuals and communities of a simpler and more just lifestyle. We must also be aware of our responsibility for the environment, the world God has entrusted to our care and of which we are merely stewards, accountable to the Creator..."

Holiness

§188. "...Jesus... preached holiness of life to each and every one of his disciples, regardless of their situation... All the faithful of Christ of whatever rank or status are called to the fullness of the Christian life and to the perfection of Christian love..."

§189. "In this call to holiness, no distinction is made between active and passive Christians, between 'full-time' and 'part-time' members of the Church, between leaders and led. Sadly many people do not grow to their full stature as Christians because they have never personally realized the challenge of the Gospel and have consistently undervalued their own potential. Yet St Paul states categorically, 'What God wants is for you all to be holy'.[1] Jesus himself said to the crowds in the Sermon on the Mount 'You must be perfect, just as your heavenly Father is perfect'.[2]

"The truth is that so great is the gulf between religion and life that even practising Catholics react uncomfortably to this call to perfection. Yet the challenge of Jesus Christ is clear. Holiness is possible... Holiness is for us where we are, to be achieved in the ordinary daily circumstances of our working lives..."

§190.   "What is this perfection or holiness to which we are called so insistently? Many find the word 'holiness' off-putting since it sounds rarefied and more suited to monasteries and convents than to homes and work places or to the routines or pressures of modern life. Others find the idea of the spiritual life a complicated one of special devotions and practices, of complex levels of prayer and of ascending scales of perfection. Yet holiness or perfection is none of these things. It is the fruit of God's grace.

"If we read what Jesus Christ has to say in the Sermon on the Mount,[3] we find that the life sketched there is a profoundly simple but challenging one. We find that holiness is not tied up with any particular calling or walk of life or with any particular stage of life.

"The beatitudes[4] speak to all, as does the call to set a good example, to respect others, to be pure, honest, forgiving and unassuming, to trust in God's love, and to treat others as we would like them to treat us. Jesus is also shown later as teaching his disciples in graphic terms[5] that entry into the Kingdom of Heaven will depend upon whether or not we have fed the hungry, welcomed the stranger, clothed the naked and visited the sick and the imprisoned.

"When Jesus was asked what was the greatest thing that God required of us, he replied that it was to love God and to love our neighbour, and at the Last Supper he gave his followers a new commandment that we should love one another as he loved us.[6]"

§192. "...In the family, in the priest's college or house, on the factory floor, in office or school or farmer's field, it is Christ's way we follow in the circumstances of our daily life. It is not a special attitude or activity reserved for times and traditional places for prayer."

A Catholic contribution?

§198. "...It may seem that the English and Welsh peoples have for a time lost their way and have become obsessed with materialistic values and unenlightened self-interest... We, the Easter People, can perhaps contribute to a renewed sense of community, of what it means to be part of a people. We can contribute an alternative vision of education from the work to renew our schools and to develop a life-long programme of Christian education...

"Above all the Easter People, by its presence and witness, can respond to the deep spiritual hunger of people, to that search for meaning and purpose which never dies completely in human beings... We can bring with us wherever we are and whatever we do the saving power of Jesus Christ, the Way, the Truth and the Life."

NOTES
[Page numbers refer to pages in this book]

[1] 1 Thessalonians 4:3.
[2] Matthew 5:48.
[3] Matthew, chapters 5, 6 and 7.
[4] Matthew 5:1-2 (see Annex 1).
[5] Matthew 25:31-46: the Last Judgement (see Annex 1).
[6] Mark 12:28-31: the Great Commandments; John 13:34: the New Commandment (see Annex 1). See also pages 24-32.

LABOREM EXERCENS

Human Work

1981

Encyclical Letter of Pope John Paul II

On most Wednesdays of the year Pope John Paul II speaks to the crowd gathered in the Piazza in front of St Peter's. If the weather is bad he speaks in a large audience-hall nearby. It is his weekly "general audience".

The crowd is usually a mix of pilgrims and tourists: pilgrims who have come singly or with friends, or in organized groups of various sizes; tourists who have a touch of pilgrimage or curiosity in them for the day. Priests and nuns are often among them but most of the crowd are neither.

When he speaks at these audiences, John Paul II often considers matters of central importance in the Christian faith; and he considers them at length and in depth, sometimes spreading his teaching over fifty or more Wednesdays. Over some twelve months in 1979 and 1980, for example, he spoke of God's design in the creation of us humans as male and female. In 1987 and 1988 he spoke over some eighteen months on the person, nature and mission of Jesus Christ.[1]

In nearly every week of the year, the Pope also speaks to the experts: to the groups of bishops, for example, who visit Rome from each country of the world in turn; to cardinals; to theologians. It is natural that with these colleagues, the Pope should address matters of particular importance for each group. He knows too that his listeners are already learned, experienced and committed in the Faith. Nonetheless, the contrast can be striking, between on the one hand, the sometimes specialist and even near-domestic content of John Paul II's talks with the experts, and on the other hand, the central matters on which he often speaks at general audiences. Perhaps the Pope is following the example of Christ, who reserved some of his most important teaching for the crowds on the hillsides of

Galilee. Perhaps he is reminding us that the most important truths of religion are not for bishops, cardinals and theologians alone.

The writing of John Paul II, no less than his speaking, provides examples of his concern to share with everyone his thoughts on central things. *Redemptor Hominis* is one example: ninety-eight pages addressed to bishops, priests, the religious communities, the sons and daughters of the Church "and to all men and women of good will".[2] *Laborem Exercens* is another: ninety-seven pages addressed likewise.

Laborem Exercens deals with something nearly all of us know about, or wish we knew about if we haven't got any, or wish we didn't know about if we've got too much: work. As its opening paragraph states, the encyclical deals with work understood in a wide sense, manual or intellectual, and including "unpaid" work at home and in the family[3] – "unpaid" placed here in inverted commas since normally, one way or another, the worker at home shares in the pay, profits or savings of someone who works or has worked for money.

The encyclical gives particular attention to the directly rewarded work of all those who depend on the rewards for self and family. Paragraphs 88, 89 and 90 show this; so do many others. Among the helpful notes in Joseph Kirwan's study-edition of *Laborem Exercens*[4] there is one in which he considers the Latin terms used in these parts of the document, terms which emerge as "worker" in English translations. Kirwan's note confirms the encyclical's particular (but not exclusive) interest in directly-rewarded work.[5]

Pope John Paul is not, however, chiefly concerned with economic value or money-value. He is chiefly concerned with the importance work can have for our human fulfilment, when the human and prime component in our work is respected.[6] Whilst acknowledging and indeed emphasizing the importance of work, for most of us, as the means of earning our sustenance, the Pope suggests that work on human terms is also important for our human dignity, growth and responsibility. He stresses the primacy of labour: the priority of human work over capital resources and technology. He sees technology as servant, men and women as master. He considers work as the means for using the earth's resources rightly, for the benefit of all; as our response to "subdue the earth"[7], the command being understood in God's way; and as partnership with God in his own continuing work of creation.

For further comment and exposition, the present author would respectfully commend Joseph Kirwan's study-edition already referred to, and the nine-page paper *The Originality and Importance of Laborem Exercens* by Professor Johannes Schasching SJ, published in *Rerum Novarum – Laborem Exercens – 2000*, the report of a symposium at Rome in 1982.[8]

Prof. Schasching presents three of the topics considered in *Laborem Exercens*: first, the danger – in some respects greater today than before – of seeing human labour as mere merchandise; second, the divorce forced by industrial revolution between human labour and family, farm, village, guild, town and other social units in which labour had been embedded, the resulting alienation which still sours us, and the potential for healing, to be found in our daily work through means such as participation, labour-capital cross-overs, and a new, more mature solidarity; third, the meaning of work for us, its true significance or "spirituality" – the "Gospel of work".

Quotation from Prof. Schasching's treatment of each of these three topics may be of interest. On the first, Prof. Schasching refers to Pope John Paul II's use of the phrase "materialistic civilization", to paragraphs 28-31 of *Laborem Exercens*[9] and to paragraph 16 of *Redemptor Hominis*.[10] The professor then continues – "A 'universal climate' can be induced in favour of exaggerated material consumption... a climate created by ideologies as well as by profit-interests. Under this pressure, average individuals are ready to accept any economic system which permits them to participate in this civilization. The desire to procure a maximum of consumer-experience becomes more important than the desire to become more human. We become ready to sell the 'merchandise' of labour in order to buy participation in materialistic civilization..."

On the second topic, "*Laborem Exercens*... does not accept the view that it is impossible to achieve social integration in the work-process but that it must be sought outside that process".

On the third, "This encyclical speaks not only about the

Gospel *for* the world of labour but about the Gospel *of* human work. This is much more than word-difference. It is an affirmation that an important part of the divine message is to be found in work itself – a message which has to be discovered, formulated and communicated... The world of work is not just a human activity in which a certain kind of moral behaviour is required. Work contains in itself an evangelical message which has significance for becoming more fully a person, more fully Christian..."

To end this introduction, it may be helpful to consider three particular terms the reader will find in *Laborem Exercens*. The first two are familiar enough, but the Pope uses them in an unusual way. The third may be unfamiliar.

Capital and capital resources

In paragraphs 30, 52-56 and elsewhere, Pope John Paul explains that by capital resources (*opes 'capitales'* in the Latin) he indicates the equipment, technology, and means of every kind that make production possible. In paragraphs 54 and 55 he uses the concept with reference to these together with nature's resources as well: "the concept includes not only the natural resources placed at man's disposal but also the whole collection of means by which man appropriates natural resources and transforms them in accordance with his needs".

Translators of this encyclical into English sometimes use the word "capital" alone rather than "capital resources" (and so does the present author) but the Pope's meaning, in the two words or in the one, is as he explains. His meaning is not narrowly financial or political.

On this and on other points, both of translation and of substance, reference to J. Kirwan's study-edition will again be found useful.

Indirect employer

In paragraphs 75 to 83 the Pope draws attention to the role of the indirect employer. In this term the Pope includes those of us who at various levels in the private or the public sector make or influence plans, policies or practices in industry, commerce, trade or finance; and the companies, the institutions public and private, the collective agreements, standards of practice, treaties and other elements of the socio-economic system which affect the situation between worker and direct employer.

Though these examples might seem to suggest that indirect employers are a relatively small number of Important Persons, the number of us in Britain who have influence as indirect employers is probably in fact very large. Consider the Pope's examples.

Those who have influence on practices in industry, commerce, trade or finance certainly include all those of us who work at board or management level in any entity of significance in these sectors in any part of Britain, whether we work in a business large, medium or small, or for a trade union, or as civil servant or politician in a central or regional office of a government department such as Industry, Trade or Treasury. We have influence if we work at board or management level in a bank or in the City of London or in an institution or association such as the Confederation of British Industry, the Trades Union Congress or the Institute of Directors, or in a trade or professional association.

We have influence if we work at board or management level for an importer or exporter; if we negotiate contracts or agreements for companies or for unions; if our job is that of economist, accountant or planner in industry or commerce; if we are a lender to business. We have influence when we invest.

There must be many further examples. To take but one: in materially developed countries such as ours, so many of us by our behaviour in our ordinary life drive the economy into ever-higher costs and prices. In our different kinds and levels of work, some of us demand high prices for the hours we give. We press for a "high-reward economy". We sometimes demand costly benefits, bonuses, privileges and pay-offs as well.

As investors, we sometimes seek high returns. As suppliers of goods and services, we sometimes seek high prices and high profits.

The number of us who make what Pope John Paul calls

"the socio-economic system" is indeed large. It's not just Them. Again and as always, it's Us, too.

LABOREM EXERCENS

Human work

§1.[11]   Work in this encyclical means any activity by humans that should be recognized as work, whether manual or intellectual, whatever its nature or circumstances. Human work bears a human signature, the mark of a human person acting within a community of persons.

The Church's teaching

§10.   The Church's social teaching finds its source in the Bible beginning with the book of Genesis, and especially in the Gospel and the writing of the apostles. From the earliest years she has considered the question of work and the social ethics required by the changing times. On the newer issues the popes developed this inheritance, beginning with *Rerum Novarum*.[12]

Fundamental dimension

§§12-15.   In his own image, God created man and woman, his supreme creation, to master his lesser creation and all its resources. Expressed in the language and thought of the Old Testament, this truth is found in the first chapter of the Bible.[13]

   Since men and women have this character and mandate, work is a fundamental dimension of human existence on earth. Each and every individual takes part in the giant process whereby we "subdue the earth" through work.

Technology

§§17-19.   Though machines do what human muscles used to do, men and women remain the true doers of all work.[14]

As an instrument we use in our work, technology is our ally, but it can become almost an enemy, for example when mechanization takes away personal satisfaction, creativity and responsibility, when it deprives many of their previous employment, or when the machine is exalted and humans are reduced to its slaves.

We must be master

§§23-24.   We subdue and master the earth because as the image of God we are persons: subjective beings capable of acting in a planned and rational way, conscious and free, capable of deciding about ourselves, and with a tendency to self-realization. Our work must serve to realize our humanity and fulfil our calling to be persons: truths recalled by the Second Vatican Council in *Gaudium et Spes*.[15]

Work corresponds to the biblical concept of subduing the earth only when, throughout the process, the human person is master.

The prime value in work

§§25-26.   In the ancient world, work of muscles and hands was considered unworthy of free men and was given to slaves. Christianity brought about a change of ideas, especially since Jesus himself devoted most of his life on earth to manual work at the carpenter's bench.[16]

This "Gospel of work" shows that "the basis for determining the value of human work is not primarily the kind of work being done but the fact that the one who is doing it is a human person". This is at the heart of Christian teaching. The dignity[17] of work is primarily in the subjective dimension, not in the objective one.

§27.   From the objective point of view, work can be valued
and ranked, but the primary basis of the value of work is the
human person who is its subject, its doer. This leads to an
important ethical conclusion: however true it may be that man
is destined and called to work, work is for man and not man
for work.

Materialism reverses the value

§§29-30.   We are always in danger of repeating the error of
early capitalism, treating work as a kind of merchandise for
sale, or as an impersonal force needed for production, especially when we live in a materialistic civilization and economy which reverse the order laid down in Genesis and treat
human beings on the same level as capital equipment – as
mere instruments of production.

Solidarity

§§33-37.   Degradation and exploitation of workers in the
nineteenth century provoked worker-solidarity. Today, whatever our social group, we should support new movements of
solidarity whenever as workers[18] we are threatened by social
degrading or by exploitation.

Fulfilment in work

§§39-41, 46.   We are all familiar with how hard work can
be: physically hard as in mines and quarries;[19] hard at the intellectual workbench of scientists and of all who carry heavy
responsibility; hard in hospitals, and hard in the family and
at home – sometimes without proper recognition even in the
family itself.
    Yet work is good; in the Latin of St Thomas Aquinas, it is
a *bonum arduum*. It is not only good because it is useful or
enjoyable. It is good also because it can correspond to human
dignity, because it can express our dignity, and increase it.

Through work we can not only transform and adapt nature to our needs; we can also achieve human fulfilment.[20]
Without this consideration we could not understand why industriousness is a virtue. Virtue, as a moral habit, is something whereby man becomes good as man.

Primacy of labour

§52 (109 end). Labour has priority over capital resources. In the production process, work is always the primary effective cause. Capital resources[21] are mere instruments. Capital[21] should be at the service of labour and not labour at the service of capital.

§§53-55. The world's natural resources can serve us only through work. Everything that comes from us in the process of economic production presupposes these resources – riches already prepared, ready for us to discover and use; riches we find and do not create. "At the beginning of man's work is the mystery of creation. This is the guiding thread of this encyclical."
In addition, we have the means by which we get and transform the natural resources, in accordance with our needs. All these means of production, or capital, from primitive field-tools to factories, laboratories and computers, come from man's labour, experience and intellect. Everything at the service of work is the result of work.

§§56-57. When we wish to make use of today's advanced means, we must first understand something of the work of the inventors, planners and makers. Work today requires ever-greater preparation and training; and whether or not a particular job needs special training, every human being who shares in the productive process is the real author or doer,[22] whilst the means, no matter how perfect in themselves, are mere instruments subordinate to human labour.
We must always emphasize this primacy of man over things, in the labour system and in the whole socio-economic system. Everything contained in the concept of capital is only

a heap of things. Man alone is a person.[23] This truth has decisive consequences for us.

Labour and capital

§§58-59. First, we must not separate capital from labour, or oppose labour to capital or capital to labour. Still less may we oppose to each other the people behind these concepts. Our work-system itself can scotch conflict between labour and capital, if we shape it to respect the human worker as the prime participant throughout the production process, whatever the nature of the tasks done.[23a]

Opposition between capital and labour does not spring from the structure of the productive process or of the economic process. The economic process shows that labour and capital are intermingled.

At any workbench, primitive or ultra-modern, we enjoy two inheritances: nature's resources, and what other people have already developed from them by producing increasingly perfect tools for us. We are masters of what has been placed at our disposal.

Our dependence in work is on the Giver of the resources, and on other people. The tools or capital may affect our work: they cannot command our work. We are inheritors, not slaves.

Economism and materialism

§§60-62. If we separate labour and capital and set them in opposition, we make errors of economism and materialism: errors of considering human labour solely according to its economic purpose, and of placing the spiritual and the personal in subordination to the material.

Contradiction between labour and capital came also from economic and social practice, when industrialization was young: we saw the possibility of vastly increasing our material wealth – means. We ignored man – the end.

We repeat the same errors now, if our thinking starts from the same theories or practice.

Ownership, property

§§63-4.   Labour and capital are not abstract concepts or impersonal forces. Behind the words are people: people like many of us, who work without owning the means of production, and others of us who act as entrepreneurs or managers, owning the means or representing the owners.

The Church's teaching that there is a right to private property, including means of production,[24] diverges from collectivism and from capitalism. In the latter case, the difference is in the way the right is understood. Christian tradition has never upheld this right as absolute; it has always understood it within the context of the right common to all to use the goods of the whole of creation.[25] The right to private property is subordinated to the right to common use.

§65 (71).   Further, property – especially means of production – is first acquired through work, in order to serve work. We must not possess our means of production against labour. The only legitimate title to the possession of means of production – private or public – is that they should serve labour, and make possible the use of the earth's goods by us all.

Therefore, we cannot exclude the "socializing",[26] in suitable conditions, of certain means of production. For certain well-founded reasons, exceptions to private ownership can be made.

§§66-69.   Exclusive right to private ownership of the means of production as an untouchable dogma of economic life remains unacceptable. Respect for work requires that the right undergo constructive revision, in theory and practice.

On the other hand, reform cannot be achieved merely by transferring production from private to public ownership, national or local. We can speak of "socializing" only when each worker can fully consider herself or himself part-owner.

Among the possibilities open to us are joint ownership, sharing in management or profits or both, shareholdings, and participation in self-governing intermediate bodies with economic, social and cultural purposes, bodies enjoying real autonomy vis-à-vis the public powers.[27]

Personal values in work

§§70-71. When we work, we want more than the pay and the other fruits, for ourselves and for others. We want to be more than a cog in a machine, more than a production tool. We want to feel an author of our work, working "for ourself", with initiative of our own. We want to share responsibility and creativity.[28]

Work concerns not only the economy but also, and especially, personal values. The economy itself and the productive process benefit when personal values are fully respected. This holds good even when ownership has been "socialized".

Duties and rights[29]

§§72-74. Work in all its senses is a duty, because the Creator has commanded it and because we cannot live and grow in humanness without it. We must work for others, especially our own family, for our country and for the whole human family.

Work is also a source of human rights for the worker, first as between worker and employers direct and indirect.

Our duties as indirect employer[30]

§§75-79.   Indirect employer includes those of us who at various levels make or influence plans, policies or practices in industry, commerce, trade or finance, and the companies, the institutions public and private, the collective agreements, standards of practice, treaties and other elements of the socio-economic system which affect the situation between worker and direct employer at home and abroad.

Those of us in industrialized countries who in our employment private or public help sustain a system of the highest possible prices for exports and the lowest possible prices for imported raw materials, for example, contribute to widening more and more the gap between the richest and the poorest countries, with effect on local labour policy and on the workers' situation in the disadvantaged countries. Finding himself in such a system, the direct employer in the disadvantaged country fixes working conditions below his workers' needs, especially if he too wishes to obtain the highest possible profits.

§§80-81. We cannot doom workers' rights to be merely a result of economic systems aimed at maximum profits. On the contrary, it is respect for the rights of the worker that must be our criterion, no matter what kind of work it is. The rights of the human person are the key element in the whole of the social moral order.

Employment and unemployment

§§82-83. All of us who are indirect employers must act against unemployment, which in all cases is an evil. We must plan and organize opportunities for work.

The overall concern of the State, and the need for coordination, should not however mean one-sided centralization in public authority. The initiative of individuals, of free groups and of local enterprise must be safeguarded.

Education and training

§86. Our education should aim first of all at developing mature human beings, and also at preparing us for an appropriate place in the world of work.

Work and employment: something wrong

§87. When we look at the human family, we cannot help noticing a disconcerting fact: while so many natural resources remain unused, huge numbers of people are unemployed or underemployed and countless people suffer hunger. There is something wrong with our organization of work and employment.

Direct employer: pay

§§88-89. In today's conditions there is no more important
way for securing justice between worker and direct employer,
private or public, than a just wage. We should judge the justice of a socio-economic system by its provision for equitable payment for work done.

Here we return to a first principle of the ethical and social
order, namely, the common use of goods.[31] In any system, it
is through wages that most of us have access to these goods –
goods of nature and goods manufactured.

§90. A just wage for an adult responsible for a family means
remuneration sufficient for establishing and supporting a
family and for providing security for its future. Such remuneration can be given either through a salary to the head of
the family for his or her work, sufficient for the family without the other spouse having to earn outside the home, or
through measures such as family allowances, or grants to
mothers.

Mothers

§91.   We must revalue the mother's role, and the hard work
of it, and the need children have for loving care to enable
them to develop into responsible, mature, and psychologically
stable people. It will be to our credit if we make it possible
for a mother to devote herself to her children's needs – without inhibiting her freedom, without discrimination, and without penalizing her as compared with other women. To be
forced to abandon this job in order to take paid work outside
the home is wrong for the family and for society when it contra-
dicts or hinders a mother's mission.[32]

Advancement of women[33]

§92.   Taking age and sex into account, we must organize
the labour process so as to respect everybody's needs and
ways of life – home life above all. In many societies women

work in nearly every sector. Women should be free to work in accord with their own nature, without being discriminated against and without being excluded from jobs, but also without lack of respect for their family aspirations.

True advancement of women requires that we do not make them pay for advancement by abandoning what is specific to them, or at the expense of the family, in which mothers have an irreplaceable role.

Direct employer: other aspects

§93.   As direct employer and as worker we have further duties and rights concerning, for example, health, safety, and moral integrity; weekly rest including Sunday at least; holiday; pension and insurance.

Trade unions

§§94-98.   The right of association entitles us to form and join trade unions to defend our just rights and vital interests as workers, within the framework of the common good, and to work for social justice. Unions are an indispensable element of life, a constructive factor of social order and solidarity.

In our unions, for the common good, we should aim at correcting everything defective in the system of ownership or management of means of production. We should see union struggle for justice as a fight for the just good, not as a battle to eliminate an adversary.

Work can bring people together. In some way, those of us who work and those of us who manage or own should come together.[34]

Just efforts to secure rights should always take into account limitations imposed by the economic situation of the country. We should not turn our demands into a kind of group or class egoism.

Nor in our unions should we "play politics". Unions are not political parties seeking power, and should not subordinate or too closely link themselves to them.

§99.   Educational work by unions offers possibilities of especial importance for helping those of us who are members not only to have more, but above all to be more.[35]

Strikes

§100.   In proper conditions and within just limits, strikes are legitimate. We should assure the right to strike, and freedom from personal penal sanctions for taking part.

But a strike is an extreme means which we must not abuse, especially for political purposes. And whatever the circumstances, we must ensure services essential to the community.[36]

Agriculture

§§101-103.   A share in decisions affecting our work, and the right of association, are as valid in agriculture as in industry.[37]

Disability

§§104-106.   The prime importance of work as something done by a human being, rather than its kind or economic rank, is seen when the worker is disabled no less than when he or she is not. The community – the authorities, associations, business, employers direct and indirect and the disabled themselves – should pool ideas and resources for training and work for the disabled, in accord with their capabilities. Disabled or not, each of us deserves respect for our human worth, and each of us is called to contribute to the good of family and community.

Migration

§§107-109.   We have the right to emigrate to seek better conditions of life, even though our move usually means loss to the country left behind, loss of someone who could contribute to the common good but instead offers his or her efforts to another society which in a sense has less right to them. But if emigration is in some aspects an evil, in certain circumstances it is, as the phrase goes, a necessary evil.

We should not exploit immigrants or foreign seasonal workers or place them at a disadvantage in working rights, conditions or pay. The value of work is bound up with the dignity of the human person.

The Christian spirituality or meaning of work

§§110-111.　Our whole person, body and spirit, takes part in our work. So as well as speaking on the human value of work and of the moral order to which it belongs, the Church must consider the spirituality of work, in the Christian sense, to help us understand how God sees work, and how work is part of his salvific plan.

§§112-116.　In our work we share in the activity of the Creator. In a sense, within our limits, we continue to develop and perfect that activity, as we advance in discovery of the resources and values contained in creation.[38]

Awareness of this ought to permeate even our most ordinary everyday work. Especially in the modern age, this Christian spirituality of work should become a heritage in which everyone shares: it should show the maturity needed to face tensions and restlessness of mind and heart.

§§118-121.　Jesus Christ, himself a worker, a craftsman like Joseph,[39] underlines that in our work we participate in the activity of God himself. Jesus gives us a Gospel of Work.[40] Though he tells us not to be too anxious about work and life,[41] his own life shows that he belongs to the working world.

In his parables, Jesus constantly refers to human work. The Old Testament refers to it too; St Paul likewise.[42]

§§122-123.　We find the Church's teaching in modern terms in Vatican II's *Gaudium et Spes*.[43]

§§125-129. There is a further aspect profoundly imbued with the Christian spirituality: the sweat and toil of work. Sweat and toil, which work necessarily involves in the present condition of the human race, offer to followers of Christ the possibility of sharing lovingly in Christ's work.[44]

Christ's work of salvation came about through suffering and death on a Cross. In a way, we collaborate with the Son of God for the redemption of humanity, by enduring the toil of work in union with Christ crucified for us.

The Christian finds in work something of Christ's Cross and accepts it in the same spirit in which Christ accepted his Cross for us. And thanks to the Resurrection, the Holy Spirit strengthens us in our work, and we catch a glimpse of new life, of the new good, like a foretaste of the new heaven and the new earth.[45]

§131. "Let the Christian, uniting work with prayer, know the place his work has not only in earthly progress but also in the development of the Kingdom of God, to which we are all called through the power of the Holy Spirit and the word of the Gospel."

NOTES
[Page numbers refer to pages in this book]

[1] *L'Osservatore Romano* publishes English translations of the Pope's addresses given at audiences general and special. Selected addresses are published in Britain by the Catholic Truth Society in their series *The Pope Teaches.*

[2] *Redemptor Hominis* (see page 117).

[3] "Unpaid" work: *Laborem Exercens* §1; also e.g. §§39, 91, 92.

[4] J. Kirwan study-edition (see Annex 2).

[5] Kirwan, pp. 74-76.

[6] Importance of work for human fulfilment: see e.g. §§22-27 and 39-46 in *Laborem Exercens* summarized above; §11 in the full text; and note 20 below.

[7] "Subdue the earth": Genesis 1:28 (see Annex 1, and page 118).

[8] *Rerum Novarum – Laborem Exercens – 2000* (see Annex 2).

[9] See page 136.

[10] See pages 119-123.

[11] Paragraph numbers are those inserted by J. Kirwan.

[12]*Rerum Novarum* (page 35).

[13]Genesis 1 e.g. verses 26-28 (see Annex 1).

[14]The true doers, or "subject" in the Pope's usage.

[15]*Gaudium et Spes*, e.g. §§12-22 (pages 69-70).

[16]Jesus as carpenter (see page 29).

[17]Dignity is used in its prime meaning, viz true worth, excellence.

[18]Work, Worker: for the wide and the particular senses, see *Laborem Exercens* §1 (page 134); also page 130 and the Kirwan study-edition.

[19]As a young man, the future Pope John Paul II was a quarry worker, and then a furnaceman, in Poland in days when mechanical aids were not all they can be now.

[20]Work as a means for fulfilment. Fr Jan Schotte comments: "Such a view enables us to look with esteem and confidence at human efforts... at solutions in which creativity, initiative and commitment to work are not penalized under a glorification of 'non-work' or of the 'meaninglessness' of work – a culture which can become a culture of the meaninglessness of life itself. A positive view of the meaning and value of work, and of hard work, is an act of confidence in humanity, and in our capacity and will to construct a more just and fraternal world." (*Reflections on Laborem Exercens*, 1982 – see Annex 2).

[21]Capital resources, Capital: see page 132.

[22]Real author or doer: the present author's words for the Pope's "real efficient subject".

[23]Man alone is a person: see also §§23-26.

[23a] Work can scotch conflict: "*Laborem Exercens* does not accept the view that it is impossible to achieve social integration in the work process..." (see page 131).

[24]Including means of production: stressed in *Mater et Magistra* §§109-112 (page 56)

[25]Right common to all: see also e.g. *Rerum Novarum* §§18-19 and notes (pages 37, 40); *Mater et Magistra* §119 (page 56), *Gaudium et Spes* §69 (page 78).

[26]Socializing, Socialization: Vatican English offered for the *collatio in commune* of the Latin. For Kirwan on the Pope's meaning, see p.68 of his study-edition of *Laborem Exercens*, and page 50 above.

[27]Autonomy vis-à-vis the public powers: see also *Mater et Magistra* §§59-67 (page 52); *Quadragesimo Anno* §79, (page 45); Intermediary bodies, Subsidiarity, in the Index.

[28]Pope John Paul II writes, it would seem, of our better self: the self that does not grab pay or profit and duck commitment.

[29]Duties and Rights: see also *Rerum Novarum* §§15-34, (page 38); *Quadragesimo Anno* §§53-75 (pages 44-45); and *Pacem in Terris* under the subheads "Rights" and "Rights and Duties" (pages 62-63): "Rights bring duties of two kinds".

[30]Indirect employer: see pages 132-134. For the direct employer, see note [29] and §§88-93.

[31]Common use of goods: see *Gaudium et Spes* §69 (page 78).

[32]The Pope here refers to *Gaudium et Spes* §67 (page 76).

[33]Advancement of Women: see also Pope John Paul II's Apostolic Letter *Mulieris Dignitatem*, 1988 (not summarized in the present work). See Annex 2; also pages 174, 178, and 183 note [12a].

[34]"In some way, those who work and those who manage or own should come together." Put shortly by Jan Schotte in *Reflections on Laborem Exercens* (1982, p.32): "The encyclical invites us to go beyond selective solidarity." See also e.g. *Mater et Magistra* §§59-67, 78-81, 82-103, 142-149; *Laborem Exercens* §§66-69.

[35]"To be more": e.g. to develop our human potential to the full. Pope John Paul II here echoes *Gaudium et Spes* §35 (page 73), and *Populorum Progressio* §15 (page 89). See also *Sollicitudo Rei Socialis* §28 (page 167).

[36]Strikes: see also *Gaudium et Spes* §68 (page 77). In 1979 a working party of British Catholic bishops, lawyers and others prepared *The Right to Strike*, a sixty-page Statement for Discussion (see Annex 2).

[37]No doubt seamen are entitled to the Church's teaching no less than landsmen, though popes seldom remember to say so.

[38]Partners to the Creator: In §§112-116 of *Laborem Exercens* the Pope refers three times to *Gaudium et Spes* §34 (page 72). He also refers to Genesis 1:4,10,12,18,21,25,31; Genesis 2:2,3; Exodus 20:8-12; Deuteronomy 5:12-14; Revelation 15:3; John 5:17; John 14:2; Hebrews 4:1,9-10; Matthew 25:21.

[39]A craftsman like Joseph: see page 29.

[40]Gospel of Work: see pages 131-132, and the second and third passages there quoted from Johannes Schasching; and *Laborem Exercens* §§12-15, 23-26, 39-41, 46, 58-69, 70-71, 112-116.

[41]Matthew 6:25-34.

[42]Parables, Old Testament, St Paul: §§118-121 of *Laborem Exercens* give some fifty references to Scripture.

[43]*Gaudium et Spes* §§34, 35, 38, 39, 43, 64, 67.

[44]Sharing in Christ's work: see John 17:4; Luke 9:23; and *Gaudium et Spes* §§38 and 39.

[45]The foretaste: 2 Peter 3:13; Revelation 21:1.

FAMILIARIS CONSORTIO

The Family

1981

Apostolic Exhortation of Pope John Paul II

Within three months of Pope John Paul's ninety pages on Work came a hundred and sixty on The Family. Readers may agree with the Pope that family and work are "two fundamental dimensions of human existence"[1] and may see these two long written reflections of 1981 as examples of his concern to address himself to the heart of everyday life. Some however may wonder why teaching on the family should come into a book about the individual in the economy.

The paragraphs of *Familiaris Consortio* summarized after this introduction are only two out of the document's eighty-six. The two paragraphs consider the role of parents in educating their children. Few people would question the inclusion of this topic in a document about the family. The present writer suggests that education of the kind the two paragraphs describe can, in at least four respects, help fit our young to lead good lives in the economy as well as in other spheres.

First, education of the kind described can foster the *development* of our children: the development of capability; the cultivation of strengths in oneself and in others; the art of bringing out the best in people.

Second, it can propose a *lifestyle*: a style that knows standards and quality, that knows the difference between on the one hand enjoying the feasts of life and on the other living in continual extravagance and waste; a style that knows how to be generous; that knows both carefulness and adventurousness; that knows money-earning without obsession; that knows Christian love in everything.

Third, this education can train in *service*. It can begin to show the number of forms good service can take – in work, for example, paid and unpaid. It can teach the value to other people at home and abroad of a job well done, and the scope for

service to those in need. It can begin to explain some of the
truths taught in *Laborem Exercens*: that when work is really
human, it's the worker who's designer and master, not the
resources or the tools; that in our work we can partner God. It
can show the meaning of commitment – of a loving commitment, in particular, in the family and at work.

Fourth, this education can train in *skills* more specifically
economic: in good use of material resources such as accom-
modation, food, clothes, money, and equipment in house,
kitchen, garden and garage. It can teach skill in saving and
investment for the good of others as well as self. It can teach
skill in assessing risk.

FAMILIARIS CONSORTIO

Education

§36.   For those of us who are married, the work of educating
our children is rooted in our vocation to participate in God's
creative activity. By begetting in love and for love a new person
who has his or her own vocation to growth and development,
we take on the task of helping that person to live a fully human
life. It is for parents to create a family atmosphere of love and
reverence for God and for other people, so as to foster the
children's well-rounded development, personal and social.

The parents' right and duty to educate their children cannot be entirely delegated to others, nor can it be usurped by
others.

Parental love should inspire all education, at home and
outside, with the values of kindness, constancy, goodness,
service and self-sacrifice.

§37.   As parents we must train our children in the essential
values of human life. Our children should grow up with an
attitude of freedom with regard to material goods, in a simple
lifestyle, understanding that we humans are more precious for
what we are than for what we have.[2]

In a society shaken by the tensions and conflicts of selfishness, we must enrich our children with a sense of justice, and

even more with a sense of love, understood as sincere concern for and service to other people, especially the poorest and those most in need.

The family is the first and fundamental school of social living. The self-giving that inspires the love of husband and wife for each other is a model for self-giving throughout the family. Everyday sharing in the home, in times easy and difficult, is the best training for responsible and fruitful life outside it.

NOTES
[Page numbers refer to pages in this book]

[1] Address at Piacenza in June 1988 on work, family and technology, *L'Osservatore Romano*, 8-15 August 1988. Likewise Pope John XXIII in *Mater et Magistra* §196: "The first chapter of Genesis relates how God gave two commandments to our first parents – to transmit human life, and to bring nature into their service. These commandments are complementary."

[2] *Gaudium et Spes* §35 (page 73); *Sollicitudo Rei Socialis* §28 (page 167).

PRAYER

1982

Address by Pope John Paul II to young people at Cardiff

To many of us perhaps, a suggestion that prayer has a place in daily life, and in the economic aspects of life no less than in others, may sound as odd as the suggestion that love has such a place. Love, and now prayer, in business? In connection with our daily work? In our producing and consuming, our earning and spending?

The present author has suggested that a cause of difficulty in seeing the relevance of love may be an inadequate understanding of what love is. Is there perhaps a similar cause with regard to prayer? Is it possible that some of us have taken our understanding and practice of prayer little beyond what they were in adolescence or even childhood – although since adolescence we have continued steadily to grow and to learn, in other departments of our lives?

Prayer does not have to use set words. It does not have to use any words. Prayer does not have to be done on your knees, or in peace and quiet, or at regular times, or in church or temple or other particular place, or together with other people, or with the leadership of a priest.

Words, posture, perseverance, and other factors such as those just instanced can indeed be helpful, and advisable too. Classics such as the Our Father, used alone or together with others in classic ways, offer us true gold. But you can also pray with a silent word or thought of your own, on your own, whatever the circumstances: at home before or after work, for example, or on the way to work outside, or amid a hubbub. A wordless thought or gesture such as a brief unspectacular opening of the hands that says, "Such as I am, Lord, here I am. Please help me to be useful today, to you, to myself and to other people" can commend to God your capabilities and your work, for the benefit of family, work colleagues, customers rich and poor, yourself and everyone else; that is, for the benefit of the economy, in the fullest sense.

The Church's teaching was recalled by Pope John Paul II when he visited Britain in 1982. For the first time, here was a Pope in our own country, speaking words chosen for us British in particular.

On his last day, 2nd June 1982, before going by motorcade to Cardiff Airport for his return to Rome, the Pope spoke for some twenty minutes to young people gathered at Ninian Park. John Paul II's addresses to young people, in all countries, indicate an especial concern to communicate what is important for life in today's world. At Ninian Park, he devoted his whole address to a single subject: Prayer.

PRAYER

"Before I go away, there is something really important I wish to emphasize... something essential to your Christian lives. It is prayer. Prayer is so important that Jesus himself tells us 'Pray constantly'. He wants us to pray for light and strength...

"It is in prayer that the Holy Spirit transforms our lives. It is in prayer that we come to know God: to detect his presence in our souls, to hear his voice speaking through our consciences, and to treasure his gift to us of personal responsibility for our lives and for our world.

"It is through prayer that we can clearly focus our attention on the person of Jesus Christ and see the relevance of his teaching for our lives. Jesus becomes the model... We begin to see things his way...

"Young men and women, when you meet Christ in prayer, when you get to know his Gospel and reflect on it in relation to your hopes and plans, then everything is new. Everything is different when you examine in prayer the circumstances of every day, according to the set of values Jesus taught...

"In prayer, united with Jesus, you begin to breathe a new atmosphere. You form new goals and new ideals ... Your dreams for justice become more definite and look for practical applications... You will discover more fully the needs of your brothers and sisters...

"It is my hope today, as I return to Rome, that you will remember why I came among you. As long as the memory of this visit lasts, may it be recorded that I, John Paul II, came to Britain to call you to Christ, to invite you to pray."

CODEX IURIS CANONICI

The Code of Canon Law

1983

On 25th January 1959, Pope John XXIII announced his wish for a General Council of the Church, which met from 1962 to 1965 as the Second Vatican Council. On the same day Pope John sprang a second surprise for anyone who thought he was just a caretaker: he announced his wish for a revision of the Church's code of law. Renewal of Christian life was the intention behind both announcements.[1]

Work to revise the code – known as the Code of Canon Law – began after completion of the Second Vatican Council. Following worldwide consultation, the new Code was promulgated in January 1983 and came into force in November of that year.

The new Code can be regarded as a complement to the teaching of the Council. It presents law for that Church which the Council came to see: the People of God, their pope, bishops and priests a leadership of service, their members all sharing in Christ's work – lay men and women as well as the leaders.

The old Code gave little attention to the laity. The new stresses the dignity, the rights and the responsibilities of all Christ's faithful, cleric and lay, and goes on to place the special rights and duties of the laity in front of the rights and duties of clerics.

The purpose of the Code is not in any way to replace faith, grace and above all love in the life of Christ's Church or of Christ's faithful. On the contrary, the Code attributes a primacy to love and grace, whilst aiding orderly development in the life both of church society and of its individual members. Its purpose is not to repress or obstruct, but to promote and to safeguard true freedom.

The articles of the Church's Code are called canons. Canons pertinent to the present work, or extracts from them, now follow without change in the English of the translation prepared from

the Latin (the only binding version) by the Canon Law Society
of Great Britain and Ireland.

CODE OF CANON LAW
From Book II: *The People of God*

Part I: *Christ's faithful*

Canon 204.1.   Christ's faithful are those who, since they are
incorporated into Christ through baptism, are constituted the
people of God. For this reason they participate in their own
way in the priestly, prophetic and kingly office of Christ. They
are called, each according to his or her particular condition, to
exercise the mission which God entrusted to the Church to
fulfil in the world.

Title I: *The obligations and rights of all Christ's faithful*

C.210.   All Christ's faithful, each according to his or her
own condition, must make a wholehearted effort to lead a
holy life...

C.215.   Christ's faithful may freely establish and direct associations which serve charitable or pious purposes or which
foster the Christian vocation in the world...

C.216.   Since they share the Church's mission, all Christ's
faithful have the right to promote and support apostolic action, by their own initiative, undertaken according to their
state and condition...

C.217.   Since Christ's faithful are called by Baptism to lead
a life in harmony with the Gospel teaching, they have the right
to a Christian education which genuinely teaches them to strive
for the maturity of the human person and at the same time to
know and live the mystery of salvation.

C.222.1.   Christ's faithful have the obligation to provide for the needs of the Church...

C.222.2.   They are also obliged to promote social justice and, mindful of the Lord's precept, to help the poor from their own resources.

Title II: *The obligations and rights of the lay members of Christ's faithful*

C.225.1.   Since lay people, like all Christ's faithful, are deputed to the apostolate by baptism and confirmation, they are bound by the general obligation and they have the right, whether as individuals or in associations, to strive so that the divine message of salvation may be known and accepted...

C.225.2.   They have also, according to the condition of each, the special obligation to permeate and perfect the temporal order of things with the spirit of the Gospel. In this way, particularly in conducting secular business and exercising secular functions, they are to give witness to Christ.

C.226.1.   Those who are married are bound by the special obligation, in accordance with their own vocation, to strive for the building up of the people of God through their marriage and family.

C.226.2.   Because they gave life to their children, parents have the most serious obligation and the right to educate them. It is therefore primarily the responsibility of Christian parents to ensure the Christian education of their children in accordance with the teaching of the Church.

C.227.   To lay members of Christ's faithful belongs the right to have acknowledged as theirs that freedom in secular affairs which is common to all citizens. In using this freedom, however, they are to ensure that their actions are permeated with the spirit of the Gospel, and they are to heed the teaching of the Church...

C.229.1.   Lay people have the duty and the right to acquire the knowledge of Christian teaching which is appropriate to each one's capacity and condition, so that they may be able to live according to this teaching...

Title V: *Associations of Christ's faithful*

C.298.1.   In these associations Christ's faithful, whether clerics or laity, or clerics and laity together, strive with a common effort to foster a more perfect life, or to promote public worship or Christian teaching. They may also devote themselves to other works of the apostolate, such as... works of piety and charity, and those which animate the temporal order with the Christian spirit.

C.299.1.   By private agreement among themselves, Christ's faithful have the right to constitute associations for the purposes mentioned in canon 298.1.

C.327.   Lay members of Christ's faithful are to hold in high esteem associations established for the spiritual purposes mentioned in in canon 298. They should especially esteem those associations whose aim is to animate the temporal order with the Christian spirit, and thus greatly foster an intimate union between faith and life.

From Book III: *The teaching office of the Church*

C.747.1.   It is the obligation and inherent right of the Church, independent of any human authority, to preach the Gospel to all peoples... for it is to the Church that Christ the Lord entrusted the deposit of faith, so that by the assistance of the Holy Spirit, it might conscientiously guard revealed truth, more intimately penetrate it, and faithfully proclaim and expound it.

C.747.2. The Church has the right always and everywhere to proclaim moral principles, even in respect of the social order,[2] and to make judgements about any human matter in so far as this is required by fundamental human rights or the salvation of souls.

C.768.1. Those who announce the word of God to Christ's faithful are first and foremost to set out those things which it is necessary to believe and to practise for the glory of God and the salvation of all.

C.768.2. They are also to explain to the faithful the teaching of the Church concerning the dignity and freedom of the human person; the unity, stability and duties of the family; people's social obligations and the ordering of temporal affairs according to the plan established by God.

C.774.2. Before all others, parents are bound to form their children, by word and example, in faith and in Christian living. The same obligation binds godparents and those who take the place of parents.

C.793.1. Parents, and those who take their place, have both the obligation and the right to educate their children. Catholic parents have also the duty and the right to choose those means and institutes which, in their local circumstances, can best promote the Catholic education of their children.

C.793.2. Parents have moreover the right to avail themselves of that assistance from civil society which they need to provide a Catholic education for their children.

C.794.1. The Church has in a special way the duty and the right of educating, for it has a divine mission of helping all to arrive at the fullness of Christian life.

C.795. Education must pay regard to the formation of the whole person, so that all may attain their eternal destiny and at the same time promote the common good of society. Children and young persons are therefore to be cared for in such a

way that their physical, moral and intellectual talents may
develop in a harmonious manner, so that they may attain a
greater sense of responsibility and a right use of freedom, and
be formed to take an active part in social life.

NOTES
[Page numbers refer to pages in this book]

[1]Page 155 draws on words Pope John Paul II used when he promulgated
the new Code (see *The Code of Canon Law* pp.xi-xv; Annex 2) and on words
of Pope Paul VI in *The New Code* (see Annex 2).

[2]Including economic aspects: *Quadragesimo Anno* §§41-43 (page 44);
Gaudium et Spes §§63-72. Canon 747 is part of the Church's understanding
of her authority for much of the teaching summarized in the present work.

HOMELESS

1987

Document of the Church's Commission for Justice and Peace

In 1987, the international year of shelter for the homeless, Pope John Paul II requested study of the problem of housing from the Pontifical Commission *Iustitia et Pax* (to give the Commission one of its longer titles). The document sifted below is a result. It was issued in December 1987.

The Commission reminds us that housing, like employment, is a part of the community's life for which responsibility belongs to every one of us, as well as to public authority.

HOMELESS

The figures

I 2.   It is estimated that a hundred million in the world quite literally have no roof over their heads, and that more than a million are homeless in West Europe (Britain and Continent.).

The people

I 3.   There are homeless individuals. There are young people who face inordinate delay and expense in finding and maintaining a decent home for married and family life. There are whole groupings of the socially marginalized.

Causes

II 2.   Among the causes of homelessness are inflated prices, unemployment, and low pay. Work should provide pay adequate to meet the needs of earner and dependents. An essential need is a place to live.

II 2.   Lack of housing is a structural problem and not merely the result of unrelated circumstances.

II 3.   At the root of the ills is unjust distribution of goods; the gulf between rich and poor.

Human right

Intro. 1, III 2, 3.   Housing adequate for self and family is a human right. The right implies guarantee of a certain degree of security of tenure.

III 2.   Far from being a matter of simple lack or deprivation, to be homeless means to suffer the deprivation or lack of something that is due. Any person or family that, without direct fault of his or her or its own, does not have suitable housing is the victim of an injustice.
    Homelessness is a structural injustice, caused and maintained by personal injustices.

Nature of housing

III 3, 4.   Property has a social function. Housing is a basic social good and cannot simply be considered a market commodity. The value of home to individual and to family gives to "housing" a meaning far beyond any purely material notion.

Action

II 2.   A just housing policy must include participation of the private sector as well as the State. It should encourage self-help projects and collaborative efforts within the local community.

III 2. Society, as well as the State, has the obligation to guarantee for its citizens and members those living conditions without which they cannot achieve fulfilment as persons and families.

III 3. In certain large cities, the number of empty dwellings would house most of the homeless. Alongside people without a roof, there are roofs that shelter no one. In such situations public authorities must establish norms regulating the just distribution of housing. This is not to say that the construction and allocation of housing can become a State monopoly. Experience where such a policy prevails shows that serious housing problems still remain.

III 3. We should give attention to building speculation in its various forms. Property is for the service of the human person. Any speculative practice which diverts property from serving the human person should be considered an abuse.

III 3, IV 3, 4. There should be participation of the different sectors of society in the development of housing policies. Alongside public authorities, and sometimes before them, private, public and Church organizations can work to remedy the lack of housing and to help the homeless. The housing programmes developed by the Church and by trade unions, cooperatives and solidarity associations are examples; also private initiatives, community development projects, and projects assisted by colleges and universities.

III 3. Lack of decent housing concerns not only the victims, and institutions, but is also a challenge to every man and woman with a house who discovers or becomes more aware of the depth of the drama of those without one. Each one of us should feel obliged to do what he or she can, either directly, or indirectly through organizations.

III 3. In addition, informing the homeless of their rights and if necessary giving them legal assistance, we should encourage them to form housing associations.

Hospitality

III 4.   In each homeless person or family the Christian must recognize Christ himself.[1] The contrast that the parable of St Luke's Gospel establishes between the rich man and Lazarus lying at his gate[2] sets before our eyes the reality of what separates those who have housing and those who do not. We know the judgement reserved for the indifference of the rich man to the needs of Lazarus. The situation of the two was reversed in the next world: and this was to be a lasting situation.

IV 1.   We must note the ever greater importance in our society of hospitality in all its forms, from opening the door of one's home and still more of one's heart to the pleas of brothers and sisters, to assuring that every family has its own home.

Criterion

IV 1.   One of the fundamental criteria for judging the justice or injustice of political and economic decisions is their effect on those on the fringes of society.

End.   The poor and marginalized are waiting for our answer, and first of all, for a change in the attitude of certain sectors of society that are indifferent to them.

NOTES

[1]Matthew 25:31-46 (see Annex 1).
[2]Luke 16:19-31 (see Annex 1).

SOLLICITUDO REI SOCIALIS

Social Concern

1987

Encyclical Letter of Pope John Paul II

Pope John Paul II signed this encyclical in the last days of 1987, the twentieth anniversary year of *Populorum Progressio*. In it he notes that the gap between rich and poor had grown even wider than it was in 1967. He warns again that for those of us who are rich no less than for the poor, development is not only a matter of material wealth or need: if development is to be authentically human, in countries rich or poor, it must engage and nourish hearts and minds as well as stomachs.

In early paragraphs of the encyclical summarized below, and more particularly in the later paragraphs 38, 39 and 40 the Pope examines the virtue he calls solidarity. He finds it linked with the supreme virtue of love.

In paragraphs 37 and 42 (and in paragraph 15, summarized below together with 42) the Pope considers the right of economic initiative, and the matter of profit. In 1988 the Pope referred again to economic initiative and profit, when addressing management and labour at Verona: "...The sole criterion of profit is insufficient, especially when raised to the level of an absolute... A business cannot do without profit. Reasonable endeavour to make a profit is connected with the right of economic initiative. But in order to be just, profit must be regulated by moral criteria, in particular by those of solidarity." Then in 1989: "The human right of economic initiative should be exercised within a social system which sees all citizens involved, in co-responsibility and participation."[1]

Popes before John Paul II have considered the nature of the Church's social doctrine: Pius XI for example,[2] John XXIII,[3] and Paul VI.[4] In paragraph 41 of *Sollicitudo Rei Socialis* (and in paragraph 8 summarized with it) Pope John Paul II adds his own analysis. He contrasts the Church's doctrine with ideology, and with "middle ways" of politics.

Among factors which contribute to doctrine, the Pope mentions the Church's tradition. Since even a Catholic archbishop has been able to misunderstand the meaning of tradition, let us end this introduction with the Pope's explanation in a matter unconnected with social doctrine but helpful when considering paragraph 41 of *Sollicitudo Rei Socialis*.

The explanation comes in a letter written in April 1988 in the matter of the over-conservative rebel Archbishop Marcel Lefebvre. After referring in his letter first to the over-progressive, the Pope turns to the over-conservative "who see correctness only in what is ancient, considering it synonymous with tradition. But", he continues, "it is not what is ancient as such or what is new *per se*, which corresponds to the correct idea of tradition in the life of the Church. Rather, that idea means the Church's remaining faithful to the truth received from God throughout the changing circumstances of history. The Church brings from the storeroom both the new and the old, while remaining obedient to the Spirit of truth whom Christ has given as Guide to the Church..."[5]

SOLLICITUDO REI SOCIALIS

Solidarity[6]

§§9, 14, 17-18.   We who are citizens of rich countries, and especially those of us who are Christians, have a moral duty to consider in our personal decisions the interdependence between our conduct and the poverty, homelessness and unemployment of so many millions of people at home and abroad: our duty of solidarity.

§26.   Today perhaps more than in the past, we realize that human beings are linked by a common destiny which we have to construct together if catastrophe for all is to be avoided. From anguish, fear and escapist phenomena like drugs, the idea emerges that the good to which we are all called and the happiness to which we aspire cannot be obtained without effort and commitment, renouncing personal selfishness.

Superdevelopment

§28. Goods, services, science and technology alone are not enough for human happiness or freedom. Unless the resources at our disposal are used with moral understanding, they can turn against us. As wrong as underdevelopment is superdevelopment: excess of material goods, making us slaves of possession, with no other horizon than the multiplication or continual replacement of things already owned with others still better. The more we possess the more we want, while deeper aspirations are unsatisfied or stifled.

Having and being

§28. There is a difference between having and being. Having objects and goods does not complete us as humans, unless it contributes to the maturing and enrichment of our being. Some of us – we who possess much – do not really succeed in being fully human because we are hindered by the cult of having; whilst one of the worst injustices in our world is that the life or being of many others – the many who possess little or nothing – cannot be human because they lack even minimum having.

Interior dimension

§29. We should not let the dangers of misuse poison the regard we have for the new goods and resources placed at our disposal – they come from gifts of God – but in trying to achieve true development we must never lose sight of the interior dimension of our human nature. Ours is a nature spiritual as well as bodily, symbolized by the two elements used in one of the accounts of creation in the opening pages of the Bible: the *earth*, from which God forms our body, and the *breath of life*, which he breathes into our nostrils.[7] So development cannot consist only in indiscriminate possessing of products, but rather in subordinating our possessing to the godlike within us.

Development

§30.   Development is not just a worldly notion. Whilst having a socio-economic dimension of its own, development is also an essential dimension of our calling as human beings, created (as the Bible puts it) "to have dominion" over other created beings, and "to cultivate the garden"[8] – powers belonging to us as means to our perfection. Today's development is a moment in the story that began at creation, a story constantly endangered by infidelity to the Creator's plan; especially by the temptation to idolatry. Anyone who renounces the difficult task of improving the lot of man betrays the Creator's plan.

§§30-32.   In the parable of the talents[9] Jesus emphasizes the severe treatment given to the man who dared to hide the talent he had received. To work together for the full development of others is today an urgent duty of every person, as well as of societies and nations.

§33.   Development would not be worthy of human beings if it did not respect human rights, personal and social, economic and political, within the framework of solidarity and freedom. True development must be based on love of God and neighbour: the "civilization of love" of which Paul VI spoke.

Obstacles

§§35-36.   Development has an essentially moral character, and so too have the obstacles: they are not just economic. "Structures of sin", "situations of sin", "social sins" are rooted in personal sins: sins of those who cause, support or exploit evil, for example; also sins of those who are in a position to avoid, eliminate or at least limit social evil but who fail to do so through indifference; of those who take refuge in the supposed impossibility of changing the world; of those who sidestep the effort and sacrifice required. The real responsibility lies with individuals.
   Today's world may prefer words such as "selfishness",

"shortsightedness", or "imprudent economic decisions" to the word "sin". All these evaluations, however, share an ethical and moral character.

§37.   Profit at any price, power at any price are attitudes opposed to the will of God and to the good of neighbour.[10] Hidden behind decisions apparently inspired only by economics or politics are real forms of idolatry: of money, ideology, class, technology. It is a moral evil that faces us, the fruit of many sins. To diagnose evil in this way is to identify, on the level of human conduct, the path to be followed in order to overcome it.

Conversion

§38.   The path is long, complex, and constantly threatened by the frailty of human resolution and the changeableness of circumstances; but we must have the courage to set out on it. One would hope that every one of us, whether or not inspired by religious faith, will become aware of the need for change in the spiritual attitudes that define our relationships with self, with neighbour, with even the remotest communities, and with nature itself – for the change in mentality and way of living which the Bible calls conversion.

Solidarity

§§38-40.   Awareness of our interdependence, a moral and social attitude of solidarity, a firm and persevering commitment to the common good, that is, to the good of all and of each individual, because we are all responsible for all; and readiness to serve – these are better than feelings of vague compassion or shallow distress. This solidarity helps us to see other people not just as instruments to be exploited at low cost but as sharers in the banquet of life to which God invites us all.

Solidarity is a Christian virtue linked with the supreme virtue of self-giving love.

The Church's social doctrine

§41. "...The social doctrine is not a 'third way' between liberal capitalism and Marxist collectivism... rather, it constitutes a category of its own. Nor is it an ideology, but rather the accurate formulation of the results of careful reflection on the complex realities of human existence... in the light of faith and of the Church's tradition. Its main aim is to interpret these realities, determining their conformity with or divergence from the Gospel teaching on human beings and our vocation earthly and transcendent. Its aim is to guide Christian behaviour. It belongs to the field not of ideology but of theology..."

§8. The social doctrine is "an application of the word of God to people's lives, to the life of society and to the earthly realities connected with them. It offers principles for reflection, criteria for judgement, and directives for action..."

Preference for the poor

§42. One of the themes of the Church's teaching is love of preference for the poor. This theme applies to every Christian; to our social responsibilities, lifestyle, and ownership and use of property. Given the worldwide dimension the social question has assumed, this preference for the poor must embrace for example the hungry, the homeless, those in medical or other need, and above all those without hope of a better future. Our daily life as well as our decisions in the economic and political fields must be marked by these realities. To ignore them would mean becoming like the rich man who pretended not to know the beggar Lazarus lying at his gate.[11]

Private property: the social mortgage

§42. The goods of this world are meant for all. The right to private property is valid and necessary, but does not nullify that principle. Private property is under a social mortgage: it has an intrinsically social function.

§31.   Part of the Church's teaching for herself, her ministers and her members is the duty with regard to what we own: the duty to use what we own, and even to sell it, for the relief of need and suffering, far and near. The Council in *Gaudium et Spes*[12] and Paul VI in *Populorum Progressio*[13] repeated the duty. "I wish to insist once more on the seriousness and urgency of that teaching, and I ask the Lord to give all Christians the strength to put it faithfully into practice."

Economic initiative

§§42, 15.   We must have regard also to the special form of poverty that consists in being deprived of human rights, including the rights to religious freedom and freedom of economic initiative.

The right of economic initiative is important for the individual and for the common good. Denial of this right, or its limitation in the name of an alleged "equality" of everyone in society, diminishes or destroys creativity. It leads not so much to true equality as to levelling down, and to dependence on the bureaucracy, similar to the old dependence of the worker-proletarian in capitalism.[14]

Development and freedom

§46.   Development that is merely economic, that ignores our cultural, transcendent and religious dimensions, cannot set human beings free: it will end by enslaving us further. We are free only when we are completely ourselves, in the fullness of our rights and duties.

Human qualities and goodness

§47.   In spite of the heritage of sin, and the sin each of us is capable of, there are in us human beings qualities and energies, a fundamental goodness, sufficient for development and freedom, because we are the image of the Creator, because we are under the redemptive influence of Christ, and because of the power of the Holy Spirit.

There is no justification for despair, pessimism or inertia. We are all called to face the challenge of these closing years of our century. The dangers threaten us all: economic crisis; war without frontiers or winners. In face of such threats, the distinction between rich individuals and countries and poor individuals and countries has little value, except that greater responsibility rests on those who have more and can do more.

Appeal

§47. "I wish to appeal with simplicity and humility to everyone, to all men and women without exception. Be convinced of the seriousness of the present moment, and of each one's individual responsibility. By the way you live as individuals and as families, by your use of resources, by your civic activity, by contributing to economic and political decisions, by personal commitment: take steps inspired by solidarity and love of preference for the poor. In this commitment, Catholics must be examples..."

§49. "In the words of a prayer of the Mass for the Development of Peoples: "Father, you have given all peoples one common origin, and your will is to gather them as one family in yourself. Fill our hearts with the fire of your love, and the desire to ensure justice for all our brothers and sisters, by sharing the good things you give us...""

NOTES
[Page numbers refer to pages in this book]

[1]*L'Osservatore Romano*, English weekly edition, 2 May 1988; 6 March 1989.
[2]*Quadragesimo Anno* §§41-43, (page 44).
[3]*Mater et Magistra* §§212-247 (pages 57-58).
[4]*Octogesima Adveniens* §4 and §42 (pages 107, 109).

[5]The letter is published by the Catholic Truth Society, ref. TPT 1988/4.
[6]Solidarity is further described in §§38-40.
[7]Genesis 2:7.
[8]Genesis 1:26-30; 2:15-16.
[9]Matthew 25:14-30.
[10]On profit, see also page 165.
[11]Luke 16:19-31 (see Annex 1).
[12]§69 (page 78).
[13]§23 (page 91).
[14]On economic initiative, see also page 165.

CHRISTIFIDELES LAICI

Vocation and Mission of the Lay Faithful

1988

Apostolic Exhortation of Pope John Paul II

In publishing an English edition of this document, *L'Osservatore Romano*[1] needed seven words to translate the two first words of Latin: *Christifideles Laici* became The Lay Members of Christ's Faithful People. The English given as subtitle, in the heading over the date, above, reproduces part of the same edition's subtitle, which in full reads: Vocation and Mission of the Lay Faithful in the Church and in the World.

The Exhortation presents the work of the Synod of Bishops who together with lay men and women met in Rome in October 1987: the Laity Synod. The document is addressed to bishops, priests and deacons, to women and men in religious orders, "and to all the Lay Faithful". Its intention is to promote awareness among lay Catholics of "the gift and responsibility they share, both as a group and as individuals, in the communion and mission of the Church".[2]

The Exhortation emphasizes the opportunities for lay Christians, through daily life and work, to help build God's Kingdom, begun here on earth. It also emphasizes that the opportunities are for women as well as men. It stresses again the dignity and worth of every individual human being. In response to points made by many in the synod, the Exhortation gives special attention to the dignity of women, additional to that given some months earlier by the Pope's Letter devoted to women exclusively: see paragraphs 49-51 of *Christifideles Laici*, below, and the note thereto.

The document refers to economic aspects of life which men and women can help improve: entrepreneurship, for example; employment; skill and solidarity at work; human management of science and technology. The Exhortation also refers to growth, of a kind even more important than growth in production.

The Church is chiefly interested in the growth of men and women; in growth into the fullness of the potential offered us by God. It is men and women who are the central resource of society and economy.

CHRISTIFIDELES LAICI

§§3-6.   The most precious fruit desired from the Laity Synod is the lay faithful's listening to the call of Christ "to work in my vineyard"[3] – to take an active and responsible part in the Church's mission in today's world.

"A new state of affairs both in the Church and in social, economic, political and cultural life calls with particular urgency for the action of the lay faithful. If lack of commitment is always unacceptable, the present time renders it even more so." As well as hopeful developments in today's world, such as a revived interest in the spiritual understanding of the purpose of life and in the understanding of suffering and death, a growing awareness of the dignity of the individual, and growing participation in work for justice and peace, there are developments even more dangerous now than they were at the time of Vatican II: claims of liberty without bounds; indifference to God; violations of human rights including even the right to life and the rights to parenthood, home and work; hunger, injustice, poverty, violence and terrorism.

The lay faithful

§§8-13.   The lay faithful are not only labourers in the vineyard: we are also a part of the vineyard. Jesus says, "I am the vine, you are the branches."[4] "Through Baptism the lay faithful are made one body with Christ... and are in their own way made sharers in his priestly, prophetic and kingly office... Our special vocation is to seek the Kingdom of God by engaging in earthly affairs and directing them according to God's plan."[5]

Baptism and its effects are important to our character as lay faithful, an understanding which can help us live the responsibilities of our vocation from God.

§14 (51). It is also important to understand the ways in which in our daily life and work we can all – women as well as men – share in the threefold mission of Christ as Priest, Prophet and King.[6]

§15. What is called "the secular character" of the lay faithful is not just something sociological: it must be understood "in the light of the act of God, who has handed over the world to women and men, so that they may participate in the work of creation, free creation from the influence of sin, and sanctify themselves in marriage or the celibate life, in family, job, and the activities of society."

Holiness

§16. The prime and fundamental vocation from God to each of us, in Christ through the Holy Spirit, is the vocation to holiness.[7] "It is ever more urgent that today all Christians take up again the way of gospel renewal, welcoming in a spirit of generosity the invitation expressed by the Apostle Peter 'to be holy in *all* your conduct'[8]..." Life according to the Spirit, whose fruit is holiness, requires every baptized person to follow and imitate Jesus Christ, in embracing the beatitudes,[9] in listening to the Word of God, in participating in the life of the Church, in prayer, in hunger and thirst for justice, "in the practice of the commandment of love in all circumstances of life", and in service, especially to the least, the poor and the suffering.

§17. Life according to the Spirit expresses itself in lay involvement in earthly affairs. Countless lay women and men in their daily life and work, unacclaimed by the world, unknown to the world's great personages, are looked upon in love by God as builders in history of his Kingdom.

The individual, alone and with others

§§28-30.   The daily life and work of the individual alone, and with others in associations and movements, can be a participation in the work of the Church. The freedom for lay faithful to form associations within the Church's communion is a right, not a concession.

An integrated approach

§34.   One of the responsibilities of a lay Christian is to testify to how the Faith constitutes the only fully valid response to the problems and hopes that life presents. We can do this if we overcome in ourself the separation of the gospel from life; if we take up again an integrated gospel-based approach to life, in our daily activities.

"To all people of today I repeat the cry with which I began my ministry as Pope: 'Do not be afraid! Open wide the doors to Christ! Open to his saving power the confines of states and political and economic systems...'"[10]

§59.   As lay faithful we cannot have two parallel lives: on the one hand, the so-called "spiritual" life, and on the other, the so-called "secular" life in the family, at work, and in society. God desires every area of life to be a "place in time" where the love of Christ is shown and accomplished, for God and for other people.

Every activity, every situation, every responsibility – skill and solidarity in work; dedication in the family and in education; service to society – is an occasion for faith, trust and love.[11]

Personal dignity

§37.   An essential task of the Church and her lay members is to rediscover and help others rediscover the inviolable dignity of every human person. Among all other earthly beings, only a man or a woman is a person, a conscious and free being, the centre and summit of all that exists on earth.

"Personal dignity is the most precious good a human being possesses: thanks to it, he or she transcends in value the whole material world. The words of Jesus 'What does it profit anyone, to win the whole world and forfeit his life?'[12] contain an enlightening statement about the individual: value comes not from what a person 'has' – even if the person possessed the whole world! – as much as from what a person 'is'. The goods of the world do not count as much as the good of the person, the good which the person herself or himself is."

"The dignity of the person is manifested in its full radiance when the person's origin and destiny are considered: created by God in his image and likeness, redeemed by Christ,... called to be a living temple of the Spirit, destined for eternal life of blessed communion with God. For this reason every violation of the personal dignity of the human being cries out to God for vengeance and is an offence against the Creator of the individual."

"In virtue of personal dignity the human being is always a value in himself or herself and for himself or herself, and as such demands being considered and treated as a person and never as an object to be used, or as a means, or as a thing..."

The dignity of women[12a]

§49. Women can be prime victims of the mentality which considers the human being as a thing, an object to buy and sell, an instrument for selfish interests. Open acknowledgement of the personal dignity of women is the first step in promoting women's full participation in life.

Opportunities for women

§51. In virtue of baptism and confirmation, woman as well as man is a sharer in the threefold mission of Christ, Priest, Prophet and King. She is thereby charged and given the ability to fulfil the fundamental apostolate of the Church: evangelization.

In addition to the participation of women in the councils and synods of the Church, "in consultation, and in the process of coming to decisions", in addition to women's participation in the Church's mission in the family, in professional life, in the civil community, and in teaching, research, and communication of the Faith, two tasks present opportunities today for the special gifts of women:

First: Reaching a better understanding of the human and Christian values in married, interpersonal life, and in parenthood; and helping men to this better understanding.

Second: Assuring modern culture's moral dimension, worthy of individual and social life; the infusing of culture and human work with a moral value.

Every human being is entrusted to each and every other human being, but in a special way the human being is entrusted to woman, who has a sensitivity towards the human person and all that constitutes the individual's true welfare, beginning with the fundamental value of life.

"How great are the possibilities and responsibilities of woman in this area, at a time when science and technology are not always inspired by wisdom and there is risk of 'dehumanizing' human life – above all when life demands a more intense love and a more generous acceptance.

"The participation of woman in the life of Church and society, by the sharing of her gifts, is likewise the path for her personal fulfilment, on which many justly insist today..."

Human rights

§38. "The personal dignity of every human being demands the respect, the defence and the promotion of the rights of the human person. It is a question of inherent, universal and inviolable rights. No one, no individual, no group, no authority, no State, can change them – yet alone eliminate them – because such rights find their source in God."

Participation in public life

§42.   A charity that loves and serves person and society can never be separated from justice. As lay faithful we must never relinquish our participation in public life, in the economic, social, legislative and other areas, to promote the common good. "Charges of careerism, idolatry of power, egoism and corruption directed at persons in government, parliaments, ruling classes or political parties, as well as the opinion that participating in politics is a moral danger, does not in the least justify scepticism, or absence of Christians from public life."

In our participation and service, strengthened by our Church life and by the Church's social doctrine, we must bear witness to human and gospel values such as liberty, justice, solidarity, dedication, simplicity of lifestyle, and preferential love for the poor and the least.

Service in the economy

§43.   Laity in particular should refer to *Sollicitudo Rei Socialis.*[13]

Universal destination of goods: private property

§43.   "In God's plan the goods of the earth are offered to all people and to each individual as means towards development of truly human life. At the service of this destination of goods is private property, which has an intrinsic social function."

Work, unemployment, entrepreneurship

§43.   The work of man and woman is the most common and immediate instrument for the development of economic life, an instrument that constitutes a right and a duty for every individual.

The lay faithful have the responsibility of being in the forefront in working out solutions to unemployment; in overcoming the injustices that come from work-organization that lacks a proper goal; in making the workplace a community of persons respected in their uniqueness and in their right to participation; in developing a new solidarity; in raising up new forms of entrepreneurship; in looking again at systems of commerce, finance and technology. We must work with professional competence, honesty, and Christian spirit.[14]

Development and ecology

§43. We have received from God the task of "dominating" the created world, of "cultivating the garden".[15] It is a task we must carry out with respect for our divine image, and therefore with intelligence and love, assuming responsibility for the gifts God gives us.

Our dominion is not absolute. Nor can we speak of freedom to "use and misuse" or to dispose of things as we please. The limitation expressed symbolically by the prohibition not to "eat of the fruit of the tree"[16] shows that we are subject not only to biological laws but also to moral ones, which cannot be violated with impunity. A true concept of development cannot ignore nature, or resources, or pollution.

Personal growth; education

§§57-58. God calls everyone to grow, develop and bear fruit. We cannot put off a response or cast off personal responsibility.

We need ongoing education. To act in fidelity to God's will requires a capability for acting, and development of the capability.

The social doctrine

§60. Spiritual formation should have a privileged place in our lives,[17] but today's laity should also have doctrinal formation. This is especially true for those who have responsibilities in society and public life. "Above all, it is

indispensable that they have a more exact knowledge – and
this demands a more widespread and precise presentation – of
the Church's social doctrine, as repeatedly stressed by the
Synod of Bishops."

Prayer

§64.   "Since the Synod was celebrated in the Marian Year...
I have recourse at the end of this document to the Virgin
Mary...:

> Teach us to treat the affairs
> of the world
> with a sense of Christian responsibility...
> You who were at prayer
> with the apostles,
> awaiting the coming
> of the Spirit at Pentecost,
> implore His renewed outpouring
> on all the faithful, men and women alike,
> so that they may more fully respond
> to their vocation and mission...
>   Amen"

NOTES
[Page numbers refer to pages in this book]

[1] 6 February 1989. The document is also published by the Catholic Truth
Society (see Annex 2). The Pope issued it on 30 December 1988.
[2] §2 (not summarized).
[3] Matthew 20.
[4] John 15:5.
[5] Vatican II, *Lumen Gentium* (not summarized) §31.
[6] Sharing in Christ's threefold mission: §14 (full text) gives the Church's
teaching on this.
[7] See also *The Easter People* (pages 125, 126-127); and *Lumen Gentium*
(not summarized) chapter V.

[8]1 Peter 1:15.

[9]Matthew 5:1-12 (see Annex 1).

[10]Words of John Paul II shortly after his election as Pope in October 1978.

[11]The Pope here refers to *Gaudium et Spes* §43 (page 73) and to *Apostolicam Actuositatem* §4 (page 83).

[12]Mark 8:36.

[12a]Pope John Paul II issued *Christifideles Laici* in December 1988. Giving a priority – as the Laity Synod of 1987 had wished – to the position of women, the Pope first in August 1988 issued a long Apostolic Letter "On the Dignity and Vocation of Women": *Mulieris Dignitatem* (not summarized in the present work. See Annex 2).

[13]See page 165.

[14]The Pope here quotes *Gaudium et Spes* §67 (page 76).

[15]Genesis 1:26-28 (see Annex 1); Genesis 2:15; and *Sollicitudo Rei Socialis* §34 (full text).

[16]Genesis 2:16-17.

[17]See *Apostolicam Actuositatem* §4 (page 83).

Annex I

THE BIBLE

Selected Passages
taken from THE NEW JERUSALEM BIBLE
published by Darton, Longman & Todd (see Annex 2)

Creation, Blessing and Command

Genesis 1:26-28
God said, "Let us make man in our own image, in the likeness of ourselves, and let them be masters of the fish of the sea, the birds of heaven, the cattle, all the wild animals and all the creatures that creep along the ground."

> God created man in the image of himself,
> in the image of God he created him,
> male and female he created them.

God blessed them, saying to them, "Be fruitful, multiply, fill the earth and subdue it. Be masters..."

This passage is referred to in *Gaudium et Spes* §34 (page 72); *Populorum Progressio* §22 (page 91); *Redemptor Hominis* §§15.2-15.4 and 16.1 (pages 117-119); *Laborem Exercens* §§13, 22-25, 113 (pages 134, 135, 145); *Mater et Magistra* §196 (page 151); *Sollicitudo Rei Socialis* §30 (page 168); *Christifideles Laici* §43 (page 181).

The Beatitudes

Matthew 5:1-12
Seeing the crowds, Jesus went onto the mountain. And when he was seated his disciples came to him. Then he began to speak. This is what he taught them:

> How blessed are the poor in spirit:
> the kingdom of Heaven is theirs.

Blessed are the gentle:
they shall have the earth as inheritance.
Blessed are those who mourn:
they shall be comforted.
Blessed are those who hunger and thirst for
uprightness:
they shall have their fill.
Blessed are the merciful:
they shall have mercy shown them.
Blessed are the pure in heart:
they shall see God.
Blessed are the peacemakers:
they shall be recognized as children of God.
Blessed are those who are persecuted in the cause of
uprightness:
the kingdom of Heaven is theirs.

"Blessed are you when people abuse you and persecute you and speak all kinds of calumny against you falsely on my account. Rejoice and be glad, for your reward will be great in heaven; this is how they persecuted the prophets before you."

This passage is referred to in *Gaudium et Spes* §72 (page 78); *Apostolicam Actuositatem* §4 (page 83); *Moral Questions* §82 (page 104); *The Easter People* §190 (page 127); *Christifideles Laici* §16 (page 176).
(In St Matthew's Gospel the beatitudes form the beginning of the Sermon on the Mount which in total occupies three chapters: 5, 6 and 7.)

Service

Matthew 20:25-28
Jesus called his disciples to him and said, "You know that among the gentiles the rulers lord it over them, and great men make their authority felt. Among you this is not to happen. No; anyone who wants to become great among you must be your servant, and anyone who wants to be first among you must be your slave, just as the Son of man came not to be served but to serve, and to give his life as a ransom for many."

This passage is referred to in *Redemptor Hominis* §21.1 (page 123) and in *Sollicitudo Rei Socialis* §38 (page 169, and full text).

(At the Last Supper, Jesus gave a further lesson on the nature of service, by washing his disciples' feet. Washing other people's feet was in those days the job of slaves. The event is recorded in St John's Gospel, chapter 13, and is sometimes re-enacted at Mass on Maundy Thursday.)

The Last Judgement

Matthew 25:31-46
Jesus said, "When the Son of man comes in his glory, escorted by all the angels, then he will take his seat on his throne of glory. All nations will be assembled before him and he will separate people one from another as the shepherd separates sheep from goats. He will place the sheep on his right hand and the goats on his left. Then the King will say to those on his right hand, 'Come, you whom my Father has blessed, take as your heritage the kingdom prepared for you since the foundation of the world. For I was hungry and you gave me food, I was thirsty and you gave me drink, I was a stranger and you made me welcome, lacking clothes and you clothed me, sick and you visited me, in prison and you came to see me.' Then the upright will say to him in reply, 'Lord, when did we see you hungry and feed you, or thirsty and give you drink? When did we see you a stranger and make you welcome, lacking clothes and clothe you? When did we find you sick or in prison and go to see you?' And the King will answer, 'In truth I tell you, in so far as you did this to one of the least of these brothers of mine, you did it to me.' Then he will say to those on his left hand, 'Go away from me, with your curse upon you, to the eternal fire prepared for the devil and his angels. For I was hungry and you never gave me food, I was thirsty and you never gave me anything to drink, I was a stranger and you never made me welcome, lacking clothes and you never clothed me, sick and in prison and you never visited me.' Then it will be their turn to ask, 'Lord, when did we see you hungry or thirsty, a stranger or lacking clothes, sick or in prison, and did not come to your help?' Then he will answer, 'In truth I tell you, in so far as you neglected to do this to one of the least of these, you neglected to do it to me.' And they will go away to eternal punishment, and the upright to eternal life."

This passage is referred to in *Rerum Novarum* §19 (page 37); *Populorum Progressio* §74 (page 94); *Moral Questions* §35 (page 101); *Redemptor Hominis* §16.9, 16.10 (page 122); *The Easter People* §190 (page 127); *Homeless* III 4 (page 164).

The Great Commandments

Mark 12:28-31
One of the scribes who had listened to them debating appreciated that Jesus had given a good answer and put a further question to him, "Which is the first of all the commandments?" Jesus replied, "This is the first: Listen, Israel, the Lord our God is the one, only Lord, and you must love the Lord your God with all your heart, with all your soul, with all your mind and with all your strength. The second is this: You must love your neighbour as yourself. There is no commandment greater than these."

This passage is referred to in *Moral Questions* §8 (page 97); *The Easter People* §190 (page 127).

The Rich Man and Lazarus

Luke 16:19-31
Jesus said, "There was a rich man who used to dress in purple and fine linen and feast magnificently every day. And at his gate there used to lie a poor man called Lazarus, covered with sores, who longed to fill himself with what fell from the rich man's table. Even dogs came and licked his sores. Now it happened that the poor man died and was carried away by the angels into Abraham's embrace. The rich man also died and was buried.

"In his torment in Hades he looked up and saw Abraham a long way off with Lazarus in his embrace. So he cried out, 'Father Abraham, pity me and send Lazarus to dip the tip of his finger in water and cool my tongue, for I am in agony in these flames.' Abraham said, 'My son, remember that during your life you had your fill of good things, just as Lazarus his fill of bad. Now he is being comforted here while you are in agony. But that is not all: between us and you a great gulf has been fixed, to prevent those who want to cross from our side to yours or from your side to ours.'

"So he said, 'Father, I beg you then to send Lazarus to my father's house, since I have five brothers, to give them warning so that they do not come to this place of torment too.' Abraham said, 'They have Moses and the prophets, let them listen to them.' The rich man replied, 'Ah no, father Abraham, but if someone comes to them from the dead, they will repent.' Then Abraham said to him, 'If they will not listen either to Moses or to the prophets, they will not be convinced even if someone should rise from the dead.'"

This passage is referred to in *Populorum Progressio* §47, (page 93); *Moral Questions* §33, 35 (pages 100, 101); *Redemptor Hominis* §16.4 (page 121); *Homeless* III 4 (page 164); *Sollicitudo Rei Socialis* §42 (page 170).

The New Commandment

John 13:31, 34-35
When Judas Iscariot had gone, Jesus said to his disciples...

> "I give you a new commandment:
> love one another;
> you must love one another
> just as I have loved you.
> It is by your love for one another,
> that everyone will recognize you
> as my disciples."

This is the new commandment of love referred to in *Gaudium et Spes* §38 (page 73) and in *The Easter People* §190 (page 127). Though enunciated in the Mosaic Law, Christ's precept of love is "new" because he sets the standard so high, telling his followers to love as he himself loved, in fullest self-giving (see pages 24-32).

Annex 2

ACCESS TO SOURCES

This Annex gives pride of place to Mass-books and Bibles.

Next, the twenty documents summarized or quoted at length in the body of this book are listed in alphabetical order, as first named in the Contents. Publication details are given. Other publications follow, likewise in alphabetical order, either because referred to in text or notes, or because they may be of interest for further reading.

The Annex ends with notes on bookshops and libraries.

A. THE MASS

Texts of the Mass in English, Latin or both, are available in ranges of editions and prices from bookshops such as those indicated below. Ask for Mass-books or Missals. Most editions include the Bible readings in full.

The Church's teaching cannot be adequately understood solely from reading. Understanding can be helped by the special closeness to Christ offered at Mass.

With few exceptions Masses are open to everyone. In Britain, unless the Mass is one in which we remember our internationally-used Latin (perhaps one Mass in four or five) or unless you stumble into a Mass in Gaelic or Welsh or for a foreign-language group, you will hear mainly or only English.

B. THE BIBLE

Translations: complete Bibles

Two of the soundest translations into English from the original Hebrew, Aramaic and Greek are the following, both reflecting twentieth-century research, both widely used in Catholic, Anglican and other churches:

I. *The Jerusalem Bible*

Published in London in 1966 by Darton, Longman & Todd. This translation is the work of French and British researchers and British writers.

In 1985 Darton, Longman & Todd published a revised edition under the title *The New Jerusalem Bible* – the edition used in Annex 1. Valuable for private reading and study, approved by the Catholic bishops of England and Wales, it may be a while before at Mass this Bible could replace the first Jerusalem Bible, now so widely printed in Catholic Mass-books.

II. *The Revised Standard Version (RSV)*

Published by Thomas Nelson, The Bible Societies, the Catholic Truth Society, Collins, Her Majesty's Printer, Oxford, and others. This is the work of American and British researchers and writers, who sought to combine accuracy with the flavour of the old English Authorised or King James version.

Two further authoritative translations are *The New English Bible* (1970) and its revision *The Revised English Bible* (1989) both published by the Oxford and Cambridge University Presses. The *REB* is the work of representatives of all the main Christian churches of Britain and Ireland, including the Church of England and the Roman Catholics.

Most complete Bibles run to between one thousand and two thousand pages. Easier to handle are editions of the Gospels alone and of the New Testament alone, available in hardback and paperback. Examples:

Gospels

The Students' Jerusalem Bible. Published by Darton, Longman & Todd. Each of the four Gospels is bound separately, with introduction, notes and commentary. First Gospel published in 1972.

The Gospels in the "Good News" version.
American-inspired simple English, published by The Bible
Societies and by Collins.

New Testament

Jerusalem Bible text: Darton Longman & Todd, 1967.
Revised Standard Version: The Bible Societies; H.M. Printers.
Further well-approved English translations are those of J.B.
Phillips (*The New Testament in Modern English:* Collins, 1972,
1977) and Father Ronald Knox (Anthony Clarke Books).

Commentaries

Some editions of the Gospels, of the New Testament and
of complete Bibles include introductions, commentaries and
notes. For the utility of these see for example page 26.
Separate commentaries are also available, e.g. the *New
Catholic Commentary on Holy Scripture* (general editor:
Reginald Fuller) published in 1969 and 1975 by Thomas Nelson
and Sons, and the *New Jerome Biblical Commentary* (ed. R.E.
Brown and others) published in 1989 by Geoffrey Chapman.

C. THE TWENTY DOCUMENTS

Apostolicam Actuositatem (page 82)
This is one of the few documents not readily obtainable on its
own in English. A full English text is however included in
Volume 1 of the Vatican Collection noted under *Gaudium et
Spes* below.
A simplified version is published by Collins and The Grail
under the title *This is the Lay Apostolate*,

Christifideles Laici (page 174)
Published in 1989 by the Catholic Truth Society.

Codex Iuris Canonici (page 155)
Published in 1983 as *The Code of Canon Law* by Collins.

The Easter People (page 125)
Published in 1980 by St Paul Publications. It is now out of print.

Evangelii Nuntiandi (page 114)
Published in 1976 by the Catholic Truth Society.

Familiaris Consortio (page 149)
Published in 1981 by the Catholic Truth Society.

Gaudium et Spes (page 66)
Translated by William Purdy, and published in 1966 by the Catholic Truth Society.

The documents of the Second Vatican Council, including *Gaudium et Spes* and *Apostolicam Actuositatem*, have been published in English in two plump paperbacks.

The more recent is published as Volume 1 of the Vatican Collection *Vatican Council II – The Conciliar and Post-Conciliar Documents* (ed. Austin Flannery OP) by Costello Publishing Company (New York), 1975 and 1984. In 1987 Costello brought out a study-edition in large format. Both editions are obtainable in Britain at St Paul Book & Media Centres and at CTS and other bookshops (see below).

The earlier collection was published in 1966 as T*he Documents of Vatican II* (ed. Walter Abbot SJ) by Geoffrey Chapman and by The America Press. This includes material dropped by Flannery, such as Pope John's *Humanae Salutis*, convoking the Council, his address on the Council's first day, and his prayer for its success. Understood to be now out of print, Abbott is available at some libraries (see below).

Homeless (page 161)
Catholic Truth Society, London, 1988; Veritas, Dublin, 1988.

Justice in the World (page 111)
Published in 1984 by Collins in *Proclaiming Justice and Peace.*

Laborem Exercens (page 129)
The Catholic Truth Society has published two editions: the Vatican English translation, 1981, and Joseph Kirwan's study edition, 1984. A shortened version is: *This is Human Work* published in 1982 by the Grail and CTS.

Mater et Magistra (page 48)
Translated by H.E. Winstone, and published by the Catholic Truth Society in 1963 and 1972. A study-edition by Joseph Kirwan was published in 1964 by the Catholic Social Guild, Plater College, Oxford.

Moral Questions (page 96)
Published in 1971 by the Catholic Truth Society.

Octogesima Adveniens (page 106)
Published in 1971 by the Catholic Truth Society.

Pacem in Terris (page 61)
Winstone's translation was published in 1963 and Waterhouse's translation and commentary in 1980: both by the Catholic Truth Society.

Populorum Progressio (page 88)
Published in 1967 by the Catholic Truth Society.

Prayer (page 152)
The address from which extracts are given is included in two booklets each of which records the texts of addresses and homilies delivered by Pope John Paul II when in Britain in 1982: *The Pope in Britain*, published by the Catholic Truth Society and *The Pope in Britain*, published by St Paul Publications (now out of print).

Quadragesimo Anno (page 42)
Published in 1960 and 1976 by the Catholic Truth Society.

Redemptor Hominis (page 117)
Published in 1979 by the Catholic Truth Society.

Rerum Novarum (page 35)
The Catholic Truth Society has published two editions: a translation first published in 1910 and many times since reprinted, and Joseph Kirwan's study-edition in 1983.

Sollicitudo Rei Socialis (page 165)
Published in 1988 by the Catholic Truth Society.

D. OTHER PUBLICATIONS

Christian Freedom and Liberation (pages 17, 20, 69)
Published in 1986 by the Catholic Truth Society.

Christian in the Material World [the future Paul VI's *Il Cristiano e il Benessere*] (pages 88)
Published in 1963 by Burns & Oates.

Gravissimum Educationis (page 65)
Included in Flannery and in Abbott: see under *Gaudium et Spes*, in this Annex above.

Guidelines for the Study and Teaching of the Church's Social Doctrine (pages 15, 17, 21, 32)
Issued in December 1988 by the Congregation for Catholic Education, Rome, published in *L'Osservatore Romano*, weekly edition in English, 7 and 14 August 1989.

Humanae Salutis (page 79)
Included in Abbot: see under *Gaudium et Spes*, in this Annex above.

Lumen Gentium (pages 119, 124, 175, 182)
Included in Flannery and in Abbott: see under *Gaudium et Spes* in this Annex, above. Also published separately by the Catholic Truth Society.

Mulieris Dignitatem (page 183)
Published in 1988 by the Catholic Truth Society.

New Code (pages 155, 160)
Catholic Truth Society, London, 1983.

Reflections on Laborem Exercens (pages 147, 148)
Published in 1982 by the Pontifical Commission Justice and
Peace, Rome.

Rerum Novarum – Laborem Exercens – 2000 (page 131)
Published in 1982 by the Pontifical Commission Justice and
Peace, Rome.

The Right to Strike (pages 80, 148)
Published in 1979 by the Catholic Truth Society.

Theology of Liberation (page 17)
Published in 1984 by the Catholic Truth Society.

ESPECIALLY VALUABLE, FOR CONTENT AND FOR READING LISTS

*L'Économie, l'Homme, La Société: L'Enseignement Social
de L'Église*
by Jean-Yves Calvez SJ, published in 1989 by Desclée de
Brouwer, Paris.

*Guidelines for the Study and Teaching of the Church's Social
Doctrine*
(1989: see above)

Social Teaching of Vatican II
by Rodger Charles SJ and Drostan MacLaren OP, published
in 1982 by Plater Publications and Ignatius Press, Oxford and
San Francisco.

Toward the Just Society
by Dennis Chiles, published in 1987 by Plater College, Oxford.

ALSO USEFUL

Authority and Freedom in the Church by Cormac Burke, published in 1988 by Four Courts Press, Dublin.

Do Justice! The Social Teaching of the Canadian Catholic Bishops, published in 1987 by Editions Paulines.

Economic Justice for all: Pastoral Letter on Catholic social teaching and the US Economy, published in 1986 by the USA National Conference of Catholic Bishops.

In pursuit of human progress: an outline of Catholic social teaching by Bishop R. L. Guilly SJ; published in 1988 by Catholic Fund for Overseas Development (CAFOD), London.

Option for the poor: A hundred years of Vatican social teaching by Donal Dorr, published in 1983 by Gill and Macmillan, and Orbis Books.

Our best kept secret: the heritage of Catholic social teaching by Michael Schultheis SJ, published in 1988 by CAFOD.

Social thought by P.C. Phan (No. 20 in the series *Message of the Fathers of the Church*), published in 1984 by Michael Glazier, Delaware, USA.

SHORT PAPERS

Christianity and politics by Dennis Chiles, published in 1989 by the Catholic Truth Society.

Economic and social affairs by Edward Booth OP, published in 1969 by the Catholic Truth Society.

Self-reliance by Roger Heckel SJ, published in 1978 by the Pontifical Commission Justice and Peace, Rome.

Social message of the Catholic Church by H.O. Waterhouse SJ, published in 1980 by the Catholic Truth Society.

E. BOOKSHOPS

Shops selling Missals, Bibles and other publications such as those noted above are to be found within or close to most Catholic cathedrals, major churches, abbeys, priories and the like.

Within fifty metres of Westminster Cathedral in London, for example, there are two: the *Westminster Cathedral Bookshop* at the side of the cathedral, and the London shop of the *Catholic Truth Society* in the piazza. Bookshops, depots or offices of the *Catholic Truth Society* or associates are in Belfast, Birmingham, Cardiff, Edinburgh, Manchester, Newcastle-upon-Tyne and Westminster.

St Paul Book and Media Centres are in London (199 Kensington High Street, W8 6BA, tel: 071-937 9591), Birmingham (133 Corporation Street, B4 6PH, tel: 021-236 1619), Glasgow (5a-7 Royal Exchange Square, G1 3AH, tel: 041-226 3391) and Liverpool (82 Bold Street, L1 4HR, tel: 051-709 1329). *St Paul Book and Media Centres* are helpful in the ordering of books British and foreign.

Good service can also be found at bookshops of Anglican and other Christian affiliation, and at bookshops in the districts of most universities.

F. LIBRARIES

Catholic Central Library

This is a lending and reference library at 47 Francis Street, London SW1P 1QR, tel: 071-834 6128. The library is behind Westminster Cathedral, near Victoria Station. It is sponsored by Franciscan friars, and is open for use upon subscription.

The library also offers a postal service. Books can be mailed to any part of the British Isles and Continent.

Plater College, Oxford

The library of this College is available to students there, including shorter-term and summer students. Plater College is in Pullen's Lane, on Headington Hill (see page 87).

In addition to Catholic and other Christian works, this library includes material from leading sources on the subjects studied at Plater College: economics, industrial relations, politics, sociology, psychology, philosophy, ethics, theology, history.

Other Private Libraries

Libraries are to be found in the houses of Catholic teaching orders (e.g. Benedictine, Dominican, Jesuit) and in Catholic schools and colleges in all parts of the country. Some of these communities and institutions have long traditions of hospitality, and allow use of their libraries to guests and students of all faiths and none. Consult *The Catholic Directory* (published annually by Gabriel Communications, and obtainable in the bookshops listed on page 198) and diocesan or local directories and yearbooks.

See also the *Guide to the Theological Libraries of Great Britain and Ireland* published in 1986 by the Association of British Theological and Philosophical Libraries.

Heythrop is a College of the University of London which has a particularly good (though labyrinthine) library.

Public Libraries

Most main public libraries include Christian material in their lending and reference sections.

Index

Names and topics of first importance are in CAPITALS. Other entries have a capital Initial. A CAPITAL or Initialled name or topic in a sub-entry may call for reference to the main entry.

EDUCATION 77
expansion: and SOCIAL Services
54
FREEDOM, Right of E. Initiative
165, 171
Growth: *see* Growth – Economic
improvement of E. life 44-46, 54-
56, 64, 75-79, 92, 93, 99 121,
135-145, 163, 170, 171, 180.
See also COMPETENCE, EDU-
CATION, HUMAN DIGNITY,
LOVE, MORALITY, PAR-
TICIPATION, RESPONSIBIL-
ITY, SOLIDARITY
inferiority 54. *See also* PAY
Initiative 51, 165, 171. *See also*
BUSINESS, ENTERPRISE,
Entrepreneur, Initiative
mentality 75
personal Initiative 51
practice, when industrialization
young 138
process 137
progress 57, 58, 75, 109, 111, 118-
122
progress: SHARING and SO-
CIAL 44, 54
Rights 52, 62-63. *See also* Human
Rights, Rights and Duties
stagnation 52
Structures and Systems 55, 121,
177
technique: not Church's work 44
welfare of the Community 45. *See
also* COMMON GOOD
ECONOMICS, the ECONOMY,
ECONOMIES
Church's concern in 13, 16, 18,
44, 67-68, 75-79, 158-159. *See
also* SOCIAL DOCTRINE
a high-reward ECONOMY 133.
See also COMMON GOOD,
Customer, Indirect Employer,
PAY, Prices, Profit/s, SERV-
ICE, Socio-Economic
HUMAN BEINGS: focus, pur-
pose 75
INDIVIDUAL'S RESPONSI-

BILITY, role 17-21, 51. *See also
throughout*
influence 55, 59
not institution of State 20
instrument, to meet growing needs
57, 58, 75-76
Lay Christians: *see* COMPE-
TENCE, EDUCATION, EN-
TERPRISE, Initiative, LOVE,
NEED, PARTICIPATION,
PREFERENCE FOR THE
POOR, RESPONSIBILITY,
SERVICE, SOLIDARITY
and Liberation
and MORALITY 44, 76, 122
purpose 44, 54, 75
at our service 75, 89, 94
and Society 54, 70, 71, 75, 76
and spiritual Values 57
State's role 19-21, 51-53, 56, 76,
79. *See also* SUBSIDIARITY
Underdeveloped Economies 53,
88-94. *See also* BUSINESS,
Capital, Capital and Labour, DE-
VELOPMENT, ENTERPRISE,
HUMAN WORK, JUSTICE,
LOVE, PROPERTY, SHAR-
ING, SUBSIDIARITY, TRADE
UNIONS, UNIVERSAL DES-
TINATION
Economism 138
EDUCATION
Christian 58, 64, 86, 125, 128, 156,
158
Church's Right and Duty 44, 158,
159
of CONSCIENCE 56, 102
critical sense 112
DEVELOPMENT 79, 92, 149
ECONOMIC and SOCIAL 58, 77
and ECONOMIC Growth 35
Family 74, 112, 149-151, 159
for FREEDOM 159-160
Individualism 112
for JUSTICE 113
Lay Christians 158
lifelong 62, 86, 128, 181
Lifestyle 112, 149

Laity: *see* Lay Christians
Laity Decree 82
Laity Synod 174
Land 37, 56
Law 97, 155. *See also* Command-
    ments, JUSTICE
Lay Christians 82, 87, 96, 125, 157,
    174, 180. *See also* Daily Life and
    Work, and throughout
Lazarus 93, 100, 101, 121, 164, 170
    188
Leo XIII 35
Liberation 17, 115, 195, 196. *See
    also* FREEDOM
Lifestyle 39, 41, 50, 59, 72, 83, 101,
    111, 112, 120-121, 126, 149,
    150, 172, 180. *See also* Con-
    sumption, Conversion, Having
    and Being, PREFERENCE FOR
    THE POOR, PROPERTY, Ser-
    mon on the Mount, SOLIDAR-
    ITY, Standard of Living
Livelihood 62, 63, 68. *See also*
    Employment, PAY, Unemploy-
    ment
"Look, Judge, Act" 58. *See also*
    SOCIAL DOCTRINE
LOVE 24-32, 58, 73, 188, 189
    aid, charity: L. is more 21, 28, 76
    in all areas, circumstances, 25, 73,
        176, 177
    best use of FREEDOM 124
    Canon Law: primacy 155
    "Charity" 28
    CHRIST'S LOVE 25-30, 70, 123-
        124
    in CHRIST'S work 29-30
    "Civilization of LOVE" 168
    CONSCIENCE 70
    in Daily Life and Work 21, 25-32,
        73, 76, 176, 177. *See also*
        HUMAN WORK: LOVE
    and DEVELOPMENT 94, 115
    "driving force of SOCIAL DOC-
        TRINE" 58
    ECONOMIC Initiatives 28
    in the ECONOMY 24-32. *See also*
        Daily Life and Work, above;

ECONOMIC, ECONOMICS,
    HUMAN WORK
EDUCATION 149-151
Equality and PARTICIPATION
    108
fire of L: PRAYER 172
"first and greatest commandment"
    70, 84, 97, 127, 188
FREEDOM 109, 124
"fundamental law" 73
GOD and neighbour 38, 70, 112,
    168. *See also* first and greatest,
    above
principle for life, work 46
head, heart 26-28
HOLY SPIRIT 68, 70, 73, 83
human qualities 26-28
INDIVIDUAL, SOCIAL 46, 68,
    70
Industry 76, 99
and JUSTICE: *see* JUSTICE
key 40
law 70, 97
legislation 108
Liberation 115
Lifestyle 83, 149
neighbour 70, 91, 98, 112. *See
    also* first and greatest, above,
    new, below, and NEED, PREF-
    ERENCE FOR THE POOR,
    SOLIDARITY
new commandment 70, 73, 115,
    127, 189
L's obligations 84. *See also* RE-
    SPONSIBILITY
open to everyone 73
PRAYER 152, 172
primacy: Canon Law 155
"prime value of the earthly order"
    109
prompter of lay action 84
and PROPERTY 78. *See also*
    UNIVERSAL DESTINATION
qualities 25-29
self-giving 27, 40, 70, 124, 150,
    169, 189
SERVICE 27, 29, 31-32, 123-124,
    169, 176, 186

PAY, Profit/s
Private Enterprise: *see* ENTER-
  PRISE
Private Ownership, Property: *see*
  PROPERTY
Production 52, 53, 55, 56, 75, 76,
  120, 137-139, 143
Productivity 75, 77
Profit/s 23, 30, 38, 43, 44, 46, 50-
  51, 53, 54, 75, 91, 99, 121, 131,
  133, 139, 141, 165, 169. *See also*
  Price/s
Progress 58, 75, 106, 109, 111, 118-
  123
PROPERTY 35-36, 37, 44, 48-49,
  56, 78, 139
  not absolute, exclusive 91, 139
  for all 56
  BUSINESS ownership 44, 54, 56,
    139
  Capitalism, Collectivism, Com-
    mon use 139
  Consumer durables 56
  Distribution 37
  divine law 37
  Earnings 37
  for Employees 37, 44, 56, 139
  equipment, tools 56
  Fair Shares 78, 121-122, 126
  for the Family 37, 44, 78
  FREEDOM, P. contributes to 56,
    78
  Homes 56, 162
  income-yielding 40
  INDIVIDUAL and SOCIAL 44,
    78
  inheritance 37
  Investments 37, 44, 45
  joint Ownership 54, 139
  land 56
  natural law 37
  NEED, PREFERENCE FOR THE
    POOR 37, 78, 91, 139, 170-171
  new propertyless 107
  obligations 37, 44, 48-49, 56, 63,
    78
  PARTICIPATION 139
  private 36, 37, 44, 56, 78, 139,

170-171, 180
  private effort, public authority 56
  means of Production 36, 37, 44,
    56, 139, 143
  Productive 37, 63
  Profit-sharing 139
  public/State 36, 139
  and RESPONSIBILITY 37, 44,
    48-49, 56, 78, 170-171
  Right 63, and main entry above
  Savings 37, 44, 45
  Selfishness: Judgment 37, 101,
    164, 170, 187, 188
  serves Labour, Work 137, 139
  SHARING 37, 40, 65, 55, 78, 126,
    139
  "Socializing" 50, 139-140
  SOCIAL dimension, function 37,
    44, 49, 56, 78, 91, 162, 170, 180
  the SOCIAL Mortgage 170-171
  State must uphold 37, 56, 64, 78,
    79
  TRADE UNIONS 39, 143
  Use 36, 37, 56, 78, 91, 170
  virtues 37, 56, 78. *See also* BUSI-
    NESS, PARTICIPATION, Pos-
    sessions, Shareholding, UNI-
    VERSAL DESTINATION OF
    GOODS
public authority: *see* State
public life: PARTICIPATION 24,
  180
Purdy, William 33, 193

Quadragesimo Anno 42, 194
Qualitative, Quantitative 109
Quality of life 62-63, 70-73, 75-79,
  84-85, 109. *See also* e.g. FREE-
  DOM, HUMAN WORK, JUS-
  TICE, LOVE, RESPONSIBIL-
  ITY, SHARING

Realities 64, 69
Redemption 115, 117, 119, 178
Redemptor Hominis 117, 194
Redistribution 121, 126
Reform 92

Church teaching 16, 44, 103
described 13-17, 57-58, 109, 134,
170
DEVELOPMENT 15, 36, 49, 102,
109, 134
ECONOMICS 44 and throughout
EDUCATION 62, 64, 86, 125
encouragement, foundation 116
"essential part of Church's Doctrine" 125
Faith and Church's Tradition 170
Guidelines 17, 21-32, 195, 196
on HUMAN WORK 134
not Ideology 170
importance: *see* Church's calls,
above
for the INDIVIDUAL 17-21, 57
"integral part of Christian conception of life" 58
"JUSTICE its objective" 58
"Look, Judge, Act" 58
"LOVE its driving force" 58
nature 14, 44, 170
objectivity 58, 102, 107, 119
"principles, criteria, directives"
107, 170
public life 180
putting into practice 58
source: the BIBLE 134 and
throughout
further sources 30, 44, 91, 102-
103, 134, 158-159. *See also*
DEVELOPMENT, above;
HOLY SPIRIT
study of SD: *see* Church's calls,
Guidelines, above
theology 170
not "third way" 170
"truth its light" 58
SOCIAL GROWTH 18, 49-50, 52-
53, 59, 63, 70
FREEDOM and RESPONSIBIL-
ITY 52, 63
Intermediary Bodies 52
personal Rights 52
State 52-53
Unemployment 52, 68-69. *See
also* ASSOCIATION, ENTER-

PRISE, PARTICIPATION,
SOLIDARITY
Socialism 46, 106
"Socialization, Socializing" 49-50,
59
Shared Ownership 139, 140, 147.
See also SOCIAL GROWTH
Society 18, 45-46, 51-53, 54, 57-58,
64, 68, 70, 72-73, 76, 79, 85,
112, 142, 159-160, 163. *See also*
COMMON GOOD, DEVEL-
OPMENT, Self-development,
SOLIDARITY, SUBSIDIAR-
ITY
Socio-economic System 133, 138,
140-141, 142
SOLIDARITY 20, 27-28, 72, 121-
122, 165, 166, 169
citizens, rich countries 84, 166
COMMON GOOD 169
contrast Lifestyle 72
contrast Equality 109
described 169
ECONOMIC Structures 121-122
EDUCATION 109
GOD's design 72
with homeless 161-164, 166
HUMAN Rights 168
Lay RESPONSIBILITY 172, 180
LOVE 169
with those in NEED 166
new 131, 136, 181
PRAYER 172
Profit/s 165
public life 180
selective 148
sense of 75
SERVICE 169
SUBSIDIARITY and S: "The
Two S's" 20
TRADE UNIONS 143-144
with Unemployed 166
in Work 131, 136, 138, 143, 177
Sollicitudo Rei Socialis 165, 195
Spirit, Spiritual 39, 53, 56, 56-57,
59, 64, 78, 83, 90, 91, 92, 115,
116, 119, 123, 127, 128, 138,
145, 157, 158, 167, 175-177,